Treatise *for* The Seekers of Guidance

Published by NID Publishers. 2008

First edition 2008
Printed and bound in the United States of America
by BookSurge Publishing.

1. Religion 2. Spirituality 3. Moral Psychology
Library of Congress Control Number: 2008933995
852-8322

Editors: Rashid Patch, and Noreen Kassem
Cover Design: Susanah I. Pittam
Production Management: Monteil Shakir

ISBN: 0-9792281-3-1
ISBN-13: 978-0-9792281-3-1

Treatise *for*
The Seekers of Guidance

by Imam Harith al-Muhasibi

Translation, Biography, Notes and Commentary
by
Zaid Shakir

Dedicated to
Shaykh 'Abd al-Rahman Tahir

CONTENTS

TRANSLATOR'S INTRODUCTION

This translation of Imam al-Harith al-Muhasibi's, *Risala al-Mustarshidin* (Treatise for the Seekers of Guidance), began in the summer of 2000 when I was privileged to do an oral translation of the book during a two-day program at the Muslim Community Center (MCC) in Chicago. The recording of that translation was produced and distributed by DEEN Inc., of New Haven, Connecticut and subsequently by Rumi Bookstore, of Fremont, California. That recording has been well-received by the Muslim community. However, it is flawed in two ways.

First of all, it is a near simultaneous translation. I read the original Arabic text and immediately translated it into English. This process, while conveying the basic meaning of the text, missed some of the more subtle meanings and implications that are essential for a sound understanding of the author's message. Secondly, my commentary on the text was very brief and in many instances entire passages were translated with no commentary at all. This was a result of the limited time we had at that program to complete the text, and the fact that a thorough commentary on the text would require access to a full Islamic library. As I was in the midst of a summer of travel at the time, I was in no position to undertake such a task.

It is out of a desire to address these two weaknesses in the oral translation, and in response to many requests for a written translation, that this work has been undertaken. The actual work on a written translation was begun by Aftab Malik of Amal Press, in the October of 2006, when he began transcribing the oral work. He was able to work through the first half of the recorded version. The latter half was completed by Dr. Noreen Kassem of Vancouver, Canada. Although I was only able to use their work as a guide to the written translation, as anyone who compares the oral version with the written one will readily observe, I am deeply indebted to both of them for their commitment to this effort. They really "jump started" the project and motivated me to do the work necessary to bring it to full fruition.

This translation is intended to serve as a layman's guide to Islamic spirituality. That being the case, the language is kept accessible and much of the jargon that usually qualifies works of this nature has been avoided. It is hoped that such an approach, from the perspective of language, will assist in rendering this translation worthy of its title, *Treatise for The Seekers of Guidance*. This approach is also befitting Imam al-Muhasibi's vernacular in this particular book. His language renders many of the most fundamental themes related to Islamic spirituality accessible to the average reader.

In this brief work, Imam al-Muhasibi presents most of the major ideas that would both serve as the basis for a full program of spiritual development and comprise an insightful overview of a system of Islamic moral psychology. He examines in great depth and penetrating insight the psychological motivations and justifications for moral thought and action and correspondingly the associated basis of immorality. In so doing, he has provided a road map that any person can follow to overcome the guiles of his fundamental enemies: the world, the ego, the whims of the soul, and Satan.

We have relied in this translation on the edited edition of Shaykh 'Abdul-Fattah Abu Ghuddah, may God have mercy on him. Shaykh 'Abdul-Fattah's work has been of tremendous help in clarifying the meanings of several difficult expressions used by Imam al-Muhasibi and in locating the source of some of the narrations Imam al-Muhasibi quotes in his text. The introduction to his work was also a tremendous resource in helping to accurately understand Imam al-Muhasibi's life and times and his position in the intellectual history of the Muslim people.

The translated text of Imam al-Muhasibi's *Risala* is presented consistently in black boldface, while my commentary is in normal type. All translated Qur'anic verses are italicized followed by the chapter and verse number in parentheses. For example, *O My Lord! Increase me in knowledge.* (20:114) Prophetic traditions are identified as "hadiths." Less brief hadiths are embedded in the text and placed between quotation marks, while lengthier narrations are blocked off and indented. An example of the former would be, "The world is a prison for the believer."[1] The references for hadiths and other narrations are presented as endnotes.

The demarcation of chapters is a fairly arbitrary process. One of the features of Imam al-Muhasibi's *Risala* is that it lacks the rigorous internal structure of many of his other works. That being the case, I have essentially divided the book into ten chapters based on length as a thematic division would be impractical if not impossible. Each of the chapters contains both a translation of the text of the *Risala* along with my commentary.

I have also tried to root my commentary on this treatise in the fertile ground of the Qur'an and Hadith. I feel this is fitting as Imam al-Muhasibi's work itself is rooted in these two primary sources of Islamic law and thought. Although

Imam al-Muhasibi makes use of his own reasoning as well as the sayings of the Companions of the Prophet, peace upon him, and their Successors, the foundation of his arguments and the bedrock of his proofs lie in the Qur'an and Hadith. This is one of the greatest reasons for his profound influence on subsequent generations of Islamic thinkers whose thought and methodology define orthodox Islam.

The production of a book is always a team effort. The author usually garners most of the credit. However, without the support and encouragement of many individuals it would be very difficult to bring any work to completion. I would like to thank my wife, the team of dedicated volunteers at New Islamic Directions (NID), my colleagues at Zaytuna Institute, and my family. In various ways they have all contributed immensely to the completion of this work.

I believe that this work will be welcomed by a wide audience. It expresses a timely message that should prove of great interest to people who are struggling against a wide array of forces that strain the spirit and try the soul. If we are able to heed the advice Imam al-Muhasibi gives us within these pages, I think it is possible for us to enhance, or in some cases reclaim, the nobility and dignity God has bequeathed unto us.

Imam Zaid Shakir
7/11/08

IMAM AL-HARITH AL-MUHASIBI

Imam Abu 'Abdullah al-Harith bin Asad al-Muhasibi was born in the Iraqi port city of Basra. No one has ascertained the date of Imam al-Muhasibi's birth with certainty. It is considered to be between 165/781 and 170/786. Similarly, very little is known about his early life. Scholars are more certain concerning his death, agreeing that he passed away in 243/857 at Baghdad.

Basra, which came into existence as a Muslim garrison town (*misr*), was established during the Caliphate of 'Umar bin al-Khattab[2]. It was joined shortly thereafter by Kufa, also in 'Iraq, and Fustat, in Egypt, as the primary military bases for the territorial expansion of the Muslim realm. These densely clustered settlements were inhabited exclusively by Muslims. They were built around a central mosque that would gradually evolve into an open university where the faithful would gather for prayers, information, and as time went on, increasingly rigorous religious education. As the conquests waned, these cities became more settled and expanded, their significance as intellectual centers eclipsing their former military importance.

Perhaps the greatest representative of the emergence of Basra as a center of intellectual activity is the great Hasan al-Basri.[3] Hasan was born and raised in Medina. However, he spent most of his adult life in Basra. During his career, Basra evolved into a city where all of the nascent Islamic sciences were to plant deep roots. Hasan al-Basri embodied the fruits that the trees emerging from those roots produced. He is considered instrumental in the development of the sciences associated with Hadith, Jurisprudence, Theology, and Sufism. The fact that, in words found in the *Shorter Encyclopaedia of Islam*, "…almost all religious movements within Islam go back to Hasan,"[4] indicates the vibrant scholarly life of the city from its earliest days, for a giant of his stature can only develop in a dynamic and vibrant intellectual milieu.

However, it is unlikely that Imam al-Muhasibi benefited greatly from the academic environment found in Basra for he appears to have moved to Baghdad at an early age. This would not be detrimental to Imam al-Muhasibi's development, for Baghdad, founded by the second 'Abbasid Khalifa, Abu Ja'far al-Mansur, was the most magnificent city on earth at that time. It reached its apex during the Caliphate of Harun al-Rashid.[5] During al-Rashid's time, the city was home to expansive and ornate palaces, spacious mosques, beautiful gardens, bustling markets, and schools of every description.

The splendor of Baghdad was financed by one of the wealthiest regimes in history. It is estimated that the wealth coming into the state treasury (*Bayt al-Mal*) annually during al-Rashid's time was 400,000,000 silver coins.[6] That wealth financed the creation of educational institutions and a system of patronage that attracted the most qualified scholars on earth to the city. Not only were those institutions centers for the study of religion, but all of the "earthly" sciences, such as medicine, mathematics, astronomy, and others also flourished.

One of the most significant intellectual developments occurring during the early period of the Abbasid Caliphate was the translation of Greek, Roman, Syrian Christian, and Indian works into Arabic. That vast literary heritage opened up the knowledge of earlier civilizations to the Muslims—in medicine, law, philosophy, mathematics, science, language, and mysticism. The efforts of Muslim scholars to assimilate that immense body of knowledge into the evolving Islamic tradition would spark unprecedented intellectual activity and fierce debates as to the proper scope of alien knowledge and philosophies in the Islamic intellectual project. Imam al-Muhasibi would be at the very center of those debates.

Imam al-Muhasibi would become one of the great intellectual figures in the history of Islam. He was both a scholar and narrator of hadith. He is said to have briefly been a student of Imam al-Shafi'i in jurisprudence. Although this claim is contested, there is no doubt that he reached a very high level of legal thought.[7] He was an inspiring orator, who is reported to have even moved Imam Ahmad bin Hanbal, one of his fiercest critics, to tears.[8] He was a major speculative theologian (*Mutakallim*), the implications of which we will visit shortly. An influential teacher, his students include some of the great figures in the early development of Sufism, such as Ahmad bin Abi al-Ward, Muhammad bin Abi al-Ward, Ahmad bin Muhammad bin Masruq, Junayd, and Muhammad bin Ya'qub al-Faraji.[9] Imam al-Muhasibi was also a prolific writer who is believed to have authored two hundred books and treatises.[10]

During al-Muhasibi's career, speculative theology (*'Ilm al-Kalam*) had gradually evolved into a science that led many Muslim scholars to formulate their theological arguments, especially those of a polemical nature, in the jargon of Aristotelian logic, Greek philosophy, and other non-Muslim schools of thought. It should be noted that it would be erroneous to describe either Muslim theologians, such as Imam al-Muhasibi, or philosophers, such as Ya'qub Ishaq al-Kindi, as Aristolean logicians or neoplatonist philosophers at this early date in the development of Muslim philosophy. Such thinkers, to greater or lesser extents, had begun formulating arguments based on the intellectual tools provided primarily by Greek philosophy and logic. However, they had not yet developed or affiliated with any identifiable school of thought.

Imam al-Muhasibi's theological approach was to intensely study the arguments of the various sects in Islam, with special emphasis on the Mu'tazilites and the Qadirites, and then refute them in their own language and style. That style was influenced by the expanding literature of foreign knowledge, but not dominated by it. Hence, like most of his contemporaries who had begun to delve into speculative theology, the main emphasis of al-Muhasibi's theology revolved around a set of well-reasoned arguments sometimes couched in the language of logic and philosophy. However, his thinking was not shaped by a well-developed and rigorous philosophical framework.

Imam al-Muhasibi's involvement in speculative theology, though limited, led to his being bitterly opposed by Imam Ahmad, one of his contemporaries in Baghdad. The main criticism of Imam Ahmad followed from a deep conflict between those scholars who relied strictly on transmitted evidence in structuring and advancing their arguments and those like Imam al-Muhasibi who felt that it was necessary to refute the arguments of the emerging sects on the basis of their jargon and methodology.

The former group posited that God revealed His Book in a distinctive linguistic style, which implied a certain epistemological foundation. His Messenger, peace upon him, articulated it in that style and enforced that epistemology, as did the Companions and the early generations of Muslims. They were of the opinion that once that style and epistemology are compromised, so too is the integrity of the revelation itself. Hence, when the speculative theologians began to adopt the jargon and methodology of the Greeks, Syrian Christians, Hindus and others, they were bitterly opposed and condemned by members of this group, whose champion was Imam Ahmad.

Imam al-Muhasibi and other scholars, who had begun utilizing those alien approaches in their defense of Islamic theological truths, opined that their course was the only practical one to take. Some of the heretical sects, they argued, were undermining the authenticity and integrity of Islam, utilizing arguments that were couched in their specific jargons and conveyed via their specific methodologies. Thus the best way to refute them was by utilizing their own intellectual tools. They further opined that an overly strict adherence to the literal message of the Qur'an and Hadith, and an inflexible interpretive methodology, did not allow for the intellectual dexterity needed to create a viable theology and thus the theological arguments needed to check the emerging sects. Hence, in their assessment, unless they acted, the impact of the teaching of those sects on the Muslim masses would be unchecked by any credible countervailing arguments.

Despite his utilization of his opponents' intellectual tools in some of his theological arguments, Imam al-Muhasibi was neither a philosopher, nor a heretic in his personal creed and practice of Islam. The following story indicates Imam al-Muhasibi's love for and defense of Islamic orthodoxy. He was born into a wealthy family. However, his father was a Qadarite, or one who rejected God's ordainment as being the ultimate determining factor in human actions. Because of this, he broke relations with his father and urged him to divorce his mother, as in al-Muhasibi's view he had left the fold of Islam.[11] He would subsequently move from his father's house, and reject the considerable inheritance his father left for him upon his death, thereby exposing himself to a life of poverty.

His stance demonstrates the depth of his personal convictions, and his firm belief that his father was astray.

Imam al-Muhasibi's major intellectual contribution was in the development of what was to become the science of Sufism, or Islamic mysticism and moral psychology. His orientation in this regard was non-philosophical. His methodology was based on the Qur'an and the prophetic tradition (*sunnah*), the sayings of the Companions of the Prophet Muhammad, peace upon him, the sayings of the scholars of the generations that followed them, and his personal insights into the states of the human soul and psyche. This methodology allowed Imam al-Muhasibi to articulate a theory of human development and salvation that focused on concepts such as fear, hope, divine grace, gratitude, God-consciousness, obedience, self-restraint, and asceticism; coupled with an understanding of devotional acts that moved them beyond serving as ends divorced from any greater moral or ethical concerns, to become a means for both personal reformation and the basis of a deeper relationship with God.

The fulcrum of Imam al-Muhasibi's moral psychology is God-consciousness as a phenomenon that manifests itself in purposeful actions. As the locus of God-consciousness is the heart, a human being aspiring to live a righteous life must first cleanse and condition his heart so that it is a fitting receptacle for the moral messages that will then allow it to properly direct the limbs.[12]

The centrality of God consciousness in his scheme is augmented by his view of asceticism. He saw that worldly detachment is necessary if we are to truly know and serve God, for the world, when overly indulged in, prevents us from His service and veils us from His knowledge. Over indulgence in the world also empowers both our lower desires and Satan in their struggle to prevent us from realizing true servitude to God. It is only when our hearts are detached from the world that we gain mastery over Satan and our lower desires and are thus able to fully serve and worship God.

Being distracted by the world also makes most humans oblivious to their sins. This oblivion in turn undermines the very purpose of life which is to obey God. Detachment from the world allows a human to focus his scattered and multiple worldly concerns into a single concern, successful attainment of the Hereafter. Therefore, it is absolutely necessary that one aspiring to deeper service and knowledge of God detach his heart from the world and limit his worldly preoccupations.

Imam al-Muhasibi also emphasized the role of divine grace in any human being's moral rectification. It is owing to the power of divine grace that the penitent servant is able to remain on the path of truth. It is owing to divine grace that the human is able to ascend to ever higher spiritual stations. It is owing to divine grace that one is able to conquer the beguiling soul. However, Imam al-Muhasibi did not see the entrance of grace into the life of a believer as an arbitrary or passive process. It is the heart that is open to receive God's grace through reflection, devotion, humility, and fostering a good opinion of God, which becomes illuminated by the light of grace.[13]

All of these themes, along with a persistent emphasis on observing the etiquettes that should govern our interaction with God, especially those related to His remembrance, trusting in Him, seeking His help, and deputing our affair to him, combine to create a powerful system of human spiritual refinement.

A notable feature of Imam al-Muhasibi's works in this area of religious thought is that they are free of the elaborate intellectual scaffolding that would qualify many later works in what would become known as Sufism. Hence, his ideas flow freely from the sources of their inspiration and are never forced into conformity to the demands of an external, predetermined and sometimes distorting explanatory or interpretive structure.

Some of al-Muhasibi's other books in this sphere include, *Kitab al-Tawahhum* (Imagining)[14], which involves an imaginary journey to the Hereafter. It would not be far-fetched to say that Dante based his work, *The Divine Comedy*, on it. He has also authored a book entitled, *Adab al-Nufus* (Etiquettes of the Soul)[15], which deals with knowledge of the soul and the etiquettes associated with its purification, taking account of its actions and states, and the means available for both identifying and addressing its defects. Another work is *Kitab al-Nasa'ih* (The Book of Counsels)[16]. In this book, Imam al-Muhasibi alerts his brothers and sisters on the spiritual path to the snares and traps that are set by the world, Satan, and the soul itself to impede the progress of the aspirant. He also provides insight and advice as to how those obstacles can be overcome.

His greatest work is considered to be *Kitab al-Ri'aya li-Huquqillah* (The Book of Guarding the Rights of God)[17]. This work is considered one of the classics of early Islamic literature, as it presents in a particularly rigorous fashion a moral psychology of Islam. Scholars who have studied it say that both Abu Talib al-Makki's brilliant work, *Qut al-Qulub* (Nourishment for the Heart)[18], and Imam al-Ghazzali's enduring classic, *Ihya' 'Ulum al-Din* (The Revival of the Religious Sciences)[19] are inspired by al-Muhasibi's *Kitab al-Ri'aya*. This should be a sufficient indication of al-Muhasibi's place in the history of Islamic thought.

Most of the themes he addresses in *Ri'aya* are dealth with in another of his books, the book we have translated and commented on in this work, *Risala al-Mustarshidin* (Treatise for The Seekers of Guidance)[20], but in a briefer, far less rigorous and systematic manner. However, one of the strengths of *Risala al-Mustarshidin* is that Imam al-Muhasibi takes especial care to build his arguments on the basis of the Qur'an and the *Sunnah* of the Prophet, peace upon him. This fact has given the *Risala* a wide reception among common Muslims, even those who do not readily identify with Sufism.

Here we would like to mention that the methodology employed by al-Muhasibi in this area of Islamic literature closely resembles that of later scholars who would expound on many of the basic themes dealt with by Imam al-Muhasibi with a very similar style. Many of these scholars are ironically identified with the Hanbali school of law and theology. If one studies al-Muhasibi's *Risala* one will find little difference between its style and that exhibited by Imam Ibn Taymiyya in works such as his commentary on Shaykh 'Abdul Qadir Jilani's, *Futuh al-Ghayb* (Openings to the Unseen Realities),[21] *Amrad al-Qulub wa Shifa'uha* (The Diseases of the Hearts and Their Cures),[22] or similar writings. Likewise, works such as Imam Ibn Qayyim al-Jawziyya's, *Kitab al-Ruh* (The Book of the Spirit),[23] *Madarij al-Salikin* (The Upward Leading Paths of the Spiritual Travelers),[24] and many of his other works, differ little from Imam al-Muhasibi's *Risala*. Sections of some of Ibn Rajab al-Hanbali's works, such as *Lata'if al-Ma'arif fi ma li Mawasim al-'Amm min al-Wadha'if* (The Subtleties of Knowledge Concerning What Each Season Contains of Religious Duties),[25] and *Jami' al-'Ulum w'al-Hikam* (The Compendium of Knowledge and Wisdom),[26] employ most of the elements utilized by al-Muhasibi so effectively in many of his works.

We have mentioned these generally conservative Hanbali scholars to emphasize the degree to which al-Muhasibi's thought was an early embodiment of what would evolve into orthodox Islamic teachings in the area of "Shari'ah compliant" Sufism. The fact that al-Muhasibi had identified and articulated the themes he deals with at such an early date, and that they were endorsed by later scholars who represented some of the most conservative trends in Islamic thought indicates that these ideas are rooted in patently Islamic sources, and argue strongly against the thesis that they are the products of alien, non-Islamic inspiration.

Our religion, as made clear by the Hadith of Gabriel, is built upon three pillars—faith (Iman), practice (Islam), and inner excellence (Ihsan). The latter is a highly desirable state every Muslim should work towards attaining. One of the definitions of inner excellence, as mentioned by the Prophet, peace upon him, is "That you worship God as if you see Him and if you fail to see Him, know that verily He observes you."[27] When we attain this state, both our life and religion are reformed, as we live and act with a conscious awareness of God's vigilant observance of all that we do, say, or think. I pray that by studying the lives and works of the scholars such as Imam al-Muhasibi, we can gain a greater appreciation of this aspect of Islam, which is oftentimes neglected, and that we are all able to harvest some of its wonderful fruits.

SELECTED SAYINGS OF
IMAM AL-MUHASIBI [28]

"One who rectifies his inner self with an awareness of God's surveillance and sincerity; God adorns his outer self with devotional acts and adherence to the prophetic way (*Sunnah*)."

"If half of humanity were to come towards me [in friendship], I would find no conviviality in that. And if the other half were to turn away from me I would feel no alienation in their distancing themselves from me."

He said concerning the hadith, "The best of sustenance is that which suffices."[29] "That is the basic provision, which comes day to day, and you do not worry about the sustenance of tomorrow."

"Anyone divested from the world finds his divestment in proportion to his knowledge, his knowledge in proportion to his intellect, and his intellect in proportion to the strength of his faith."

"Knowledge bequeaths fear, divestment from the world bequeaths comfort, and gnosis bequeaths self criticism."

"The basis of obedience is impeccability. The basis of impeccability is God-consciousness. The basis of God-consciousness is [balancing between] fear and hope, and the basis of those two is knowledge of the promise and the threat."

"Good character is bearing abuse, rarely becoming angry, a pleasant face, and sweet speech."

"Everything has an essence. The essence of a human being is his intellect, and the essence of his intellect is patience."

"If you do not hear the caller to God, how can you answer his call?"

"The oppressor is remorseful[30] even if people praise him. The oppressed is safe even if people condemn him. The content person is wealthy even if he is hungry. And the covetous person is impoverished even if he owns [plenty]."

"One who does not thank God for a blessing has called for its eradication."

"The best person is one who does not allow his Hereafter to preoccupy him from his worldly affair, nor does he allow his worldly affair to preoccupy him from his Hereafter."

"The tribulation of the seeker of the world is the idling of his heart from remembrance of the Hereafter."

"Whoever emerges from the authority of fear into the haughtiness of security [from God's decree], the paths leading to the places of [his] ruin have been greatly expanded."

"People differ in worldly divestment in proportion to the soundness of [their] intellects, and the purity of [their] hearts. The most virtuous are the most intelligent and those who best understand God."

In the Name of God, Most Merciful, Most
Compassionate

CHAPTER ONE

All praise is fittingly rendered unto God, the First, the
Preexisting,[31] the One, and the Majestic.

Something can be first and also have a beginning. Adam
was the first man, but he had a beginning. God is unique
in that He is the first with no beginning. His existence
necessarily precedes all other existence, and all else in existence owes its existence to Him, the Creator. Hence, He alone
is preexisting. One holding this unique distinction is deserving of all praise for all else owes its existence to Him. This is
the foundation of the most credible arguments for the existence of God. Acknowledging God as preexisting and eternal
allows us to avoid the logical problems arising from infinite
regress, when trying to account for the origin of creation, and
the appearance of an obvious effect, in this case, the creation,
without the existence of a causal agent, the creator.

He has no likeness or equal. I praise Him in a manner
befitting the extent of His blessings, in a manner that
reflects the expansiveness of His bounties.

In other words, I praise Him in a manner that defies the limitations of human descriptive powers. If we were to enumerate the blessings of God we could not count them, as God mentions in the Qur'an. (14:34) Hence, what Imam al-Muhasibi is saying is that he praises God in a fashion that has no limitations.

I bear witness that there is no deity but God, He is alone, He has no partners. [This is] the testimony of one who knows His Lordship, who realizes His Oneness.

It is important to note that even at this early date the terms *rububiyya* (God's Lordship) and *'ilahiyya* were used by recognized Muslim scholars. These are not terms introduced by latter scholars such as Ibn Taymiyya, as some people allege. Here, approximately two hundred years after the Prophet, peace upon him, we find these terms being employed by scholars such as Imam al-Muhasibi. However, the way these terms were subsequently used may involve varying degrees of controversy.

I bear witness that Muhammad is His Servant and His Messenger.

The description of the perfect servitude of Muhammad, peace upon him, is the highest honor bestowed upon him. Hence, when God, Most High, mentions in the Qur'an the moments when He has exalted the Prophet, peace upon him, and bestowed upon him blessings not given to anyone else, it is in the context of his servitude. For example, *All praise is fittingly for God who has revealed unto His servant the scripture.* (18:1).

Similarly, when He mentions the Night Journey (*Isra'*), He mentions it in the context of the servitude of the Prophet,

All Praise is for God who has carried His servant by night from the Sacred Mosque to the Furthest Mosque, whose precincts He has blessed... (17:1). This divinely guided journey happened in the aftermath of the debacle at Ta'if, where the Prophet, peace upon Him, had suffered greatly. The painful affair occurring at Ta'if occurred in the aftermath of the severe boycott inflicted on him and his followers by the Quraysh, during which his protector, Abu Talib, and his beloved wife, Khadija, passed away.

Through this journey, God consoled Him and reassured him by letting him know that his standing with God remained lofty. Hence, God places emphasis on his servitude, peace upon him. This is the highest station that humans can aspire to attain—the station of perfect servitude. For the more perfect our servitude, the more exalted the Lordship of God is with us.

As believers we want to be servants of God for we recognize that it is our servitude to God that liberates us from servitude to all else. God reminds us that this is the rationale governing our creation. He mentions in the Qur'an, *I have only created the Jinn and Humans that they serve me.* (51:56).

He has chosen him to be the recipient of His {final} revelation. Furthermore, He sealed the prophetic office after sending him. He has made him a proof against all of humanity. *...in order that those who perish will perish having a clear proof established against them, and those who live on will do so with a clear proof established for them.* (8:42).

This verse was revealed concerning the Battle of Badr. The disbelievers saw how God, Most High, had arranged things, that He had sent rain the previous night and bogged them down in a muddy quagmire. That same downpour gave the Muslims drink, yet they were spared the hardships that burdened the disbelievers. The disbelievers saw how God, Most High, had arranged the forces so that they were cut off from the wells of Badr, while the Muslims had control of those sources of water. God had made the disbelievers' numbers seem small in the eyes of the Muslims, thus encouraging them. Correspondingly, He had made the Muslims' number seem large in the eyes of the disbelievers, discouraging them. After all these divine arrangements, those who perished, knew that this was the work of God, and those who lived knew that their victory was due to God.

Hence, Imam al-Muhasibi uses this verse as a proof to indicate to those who reject this faith, that indeed this religion is true, in order that they have no argument with God on the Day of Judgment. As for those who accept it, they do so based on clear proofs and evidences. Thus, they will live on the basis of that proof and evidence, both in this world and the next. Who has established this proof on God's behalf among the human family? It was established by Muhammad, the Messenger of God, peace upon him.

You should know that God has chosen from His believing servants those intelligent folk who know Him and acknowledge His Command. He has described them as being faithful, virtuous, fearful, and reverent.

The testimony of our religion lies in our character. Are we patient when inflicted with adversity? Are we truthful in our dealings? Are we faithful in all of our relationships—with God, with ourselves, and with our fellow humans? These are the types of questions we need to be asking; for they are the types of questions that push us towards the attainment of higher moral and ethical standards.

The difference between fear (*khauf*) and reverence (*khashya*) is that the latter is borne from awe. Being in awe of something is not associated with dread or apprehension, which are sources of fear. Rather, awe is evoked by the beauty or grandeur of a presence or reality. This is the difference between the two. However, both are relevant in our relationship with God and both provide motivations for us to obey His commandments and to avoid His prohibitions.

Rather, those possessing intellects are mindful. Those who are faithful to the covenant they have convened with God, and do not breech the oath. Those who join what God has commanded to be joined; they reverence their Lord, and they fear a terrible accounting. (13:19-21)

We enter into a covenant with God when we make the declaration of faith by saying, There is no god, but God. Muhammad is the Messenger of God (*La ilaha illallah, Muhammadan Rasulullah*). In so doing, we accept to live the life of a Muslim, to strive to obey the commandments of God and to avoid those things He has prohibited. We also enter into a covenant with ourselves; we are vowing that we will not oppress our souls by exposing them to ruin and damnation. Furthermore, we are entering into a covenant with our fellow human beings. We are pledging to devote ourselves to their service, not to say or do anything that will jeopardize their wellbeing and security, to work for the common good, and to protect their lives, property and honor.

God mentions in the Qur'an that there are people who are truthful in the covenant they have entered into and that they do not breach it. In fact, they are willing to sacrifice their very lives to uphold its sanctity. He says, *Among the believers are men who are truthful in the covenant they have convened with God. Among them are those who have already fulfilled it, and others who are waiting, and they have never wavered.* (33:23)

Those who join what God has commanded to be joined.

Those who join what God has commanded to be joined keep healthy blood-ties by maintaining good relations with their kith and kin. They realize the importance of family ties and the essential nature of the family in human societies. They also realize that the family is a divinely ordained, divinely sanctified institution. All of these meanings are summarized in the verse, *O Humankind! Fear your Lord who has created you from a single soul and from that soul has made its mate, and from those two has sent forth multitudes of men and women. Fear your Lord by whom you will be asked concerning the sanctity of the relationships emanating from the womb. Verily, God ever watches over you.* (4:1)

God also mentions in the Qur'an, *O believers! Fear God as He should rightfully be feared and die not except as Muslims.* (3:101) Similarly, *Do not fear them* [Satan and his dupes]; *rather fear me if indeed you are believers.* (3:175) These narrations move us to understand that religion will never be sound without a real and present fear of God. However, as we shall subsequently see, that fear has to be balanced by a longing for God's mercy. The incumbency of balancing between fear and hope is one of the fundamental concepts in the moral psychology of Islam.

Those whose breasts God has expanded, by allowing them to confirm the truth in their hearts, to long for the means that lead to Him, and to adhere to the way of those possessing intellects by carefully minding the limits established by the divine law.

It is related that a desert Arab asked the Messenger of God, peace upon him, "Who is the best of all people?" He responded, "One who is blessed with a long life accompanied with good deeds."[32] One given these two things, a long life filled with righteous deeds has truly been blessed.

What are the means that lead to God? Those means are all of the things that lead you, or draw you near, to God, Most High. Obeying His commandments, avoiding His prohibitions, reciting and acting on His scripture, engaging in His remembrance, worshipping Him as He commanded us to do on the basis of knowledge and truth, seeking the assistance of righteous, learned Muslims, sitting in the company of pious people, praying to God that He helps us; all of these are valid means that lead to God. Some scholars have described other means that might be deemed controversial. What we have mentioned here is sufficient, for cautiousness in dealing with controversial matters is one of the best manifestations of true religiosity.

God mentions in the Qur'an, *O Believers! Be dutifully mindful of God and pursue the means that lead unto Him; strenuously exert yourselves for His sake in order to be successful.* (5:35) In this verse, we are reminded that the essence of God-consciousness lies in leaving off harmful and forbidden things, even though the soul may have a deep craving for them. The essence of pursuing the means to God lies in doing those things He has commanded, even though the soul may find those things difficult and undesirable. Hence, we are commanded to exert ourselves strenuously, because the path the believer walks in this world is a difficult one and one has to work arduously to remain on it.[33]

You will note that Imam al-Muhasibi frequently emphasizes the intellect, because it is the quality that elevates humans above the "dumb" animals. The intellect is what allows us to worship God on the basis of sound knowledge. Hence, the intellect is the locus of religious responsibility. For this reason, a person that has lost his intellect is not religiously responsible for his actions. If a person goes mad, forgets, or is sleeping he is not conscious of his actions. If in such a state he violates God's ordainments, he is not religiously responsible because he does not have control over his intellect. The Prophet, peace upon him, informed us, "God has relieved my community of unintended errors, forgetfulness, and transgressions committed under compulsion."[34]

[Those limits] have been demarcated by the Book of God, Most High, the Way of His Messenger, peace upon him, and what the Rightly Guided Imams have agreed on. This is the straight path that God has called his servants to. God says in His Book, *This is My straight path, so follow it. Do not follow divergent paths that lead you away from His Path. Thus have you been admonished in order to obtain God-consciousness.* **(6:153)**

The Messenger of God mentioned, "It is incumbent upon you to adhere to my Way and the way the Rightly Guided Successors, bite into them with your hind teeth."[35]

This section of the text raises very critical points. There is little dispute, in theory, between Muslims concerning the incumbency of following the Prophet, peace upon him. The injunctions in the Qur'an and the prophetic tradition urging us to follow him are too many and too strong to be ignored. For example, God mentions in the Qur'an, *Say!*[36] *If indeed you love God then follow me. God will then love you and forgive your sins. And God is Forgiving, Merciful.* (3:31) Similarly, *I swear by Your Lord! They do not truly believe until they make you the judge in all of the disputes occurring between them, and then find no agitation concerning what you have adjudicated, and they submit totally to it.* (4:65) Likewise, *If you differ in a matter then refer it back to God and the Messenger...* (4:59)

However, Muslims do differ concerning the incumbency of following the way of the Rightly Guided Successors: Abu

Bakr, 'Umar, 'Uthman, and 'Ali. What many fail to understand is that the Way of the Rightly Guided Successors is the
Way of the Prophet, peace upon him, when rulings issued
by the Successors have been confirmed by binding scholarly
consensus (*Ijma'*). In that case, their way becomes a source of
binding legislation. The Prophet, peace upon him, as mentioned above, declared, "It is incumbent upon you to follow
my way and the way of my Rightly Guided Successors, bite
into it with your hind teeth."[37]

After mentioning the importance of adherence to the prophetic way, Imam al-Muhasibi reminds us of basic obligations
towards the Qur'an. This is a very important section, as Imam
al-Muhasibi is giving us the methodology of those Muslims
who want to be truthful in the way they engage in with the
Book of God.

**Know that the obligation owed to the book of God
is to act on the basis of the rulings conveyed by its
commandments and prohibitions; to respond to its
threats with fear, to its promises with longing, to
[have] faith concerning the truthfulness of its obscure
statements, and to reflect on its stories and parables.**

This helps us to maintain a healthy level of fear of God. By
balancing between fear and hope we are neither overwhelmed
by hope for God's mercy such that we take it for granted, nor
are we overwhelmed by fear, and thereby despair, and come to
believe that our devotion or repentance will not avail us with
God. Both of these themes will be discussed in detail later in
the book. Here the Imam is introducing some basic concepts.

The obscure statements in the Qur'an might confuse us.
God mentions, for example that *The Hand of God is above their
hands.* (48:10) However, He also says, *There is nothing like unto
Him.* (42:11) Therefore, the first verse cannot mean that God

has a physical hand that is physically over their hands. If that were that the case, there would be something *like unto Him.* What exactly does the expression mean? We do not know. We depute that knowledge to God, but we believe in the veracity of the statement as it has been related to us in the scripture. This is what Imam al-Muhasibi means when he urges us to believe in those obscure scriptural statements. One of the safest positions concerning such verses is conveyed to us from Imam Shafi'i. It is related that he said, "I believe in God and in what comes to us from God as God intended it. And I believe in the Messenger of God and in what comes to us from the Messenger of God as he intended it."[38]

Just as we should act on the commandments and prohibitions contained in the Qur'an, just as we should long for what it promises us, and be fearful of its threats, we should also reflect deeply on its stories and parables. We should try to identify the themes of those stories such as oppression, the struggle of good and evil in the world, the reward of humility and the dangers of arrogance, the rewards of obedience to God and the painful consequences of rebellion, and the destiny of man. All of these are themes that make the Qur'an such a profound and enduring work. However, when we fail to reflect on the Qur'an, in many instances we miss its profundity. God mentions, *Do they not reflect on the Qur'an, or are seals on their hearts?* (47:24)

If you do these things you have emerged from the darkness of ignorance into the light of knowledge, and from the torment of doubt into the comfort of certitude.

If we take this approach in dealing with the Qur'an and interacting with its message, we would have rendered a great service to our souls. In so doing we would have taken a huge step in bringing our souls from the darkness of misguidance into the light of truth. God refers to His scripture as a light, *O Humanity! There has come to you from your Lord a proof and a clear light.* (4:174)

Islam is also a light He has sent to guide us through the darkness of this world and to share with others. It is incumbent upon us to shine that light. When we approach Islam as merely a set of regulations we are enjoined to obey, we can remove the sweetness of the faith from our hearts. This is indicated by the prophetic tradition which mentions that a man came to the Prophet, peace upon him, and complained that the legalistic aspects of the faith were burdening him. The Prophet, peace upon him, responded, "Do not let a moment pass except that your tongue is moist with the remembrance of God."[39]

If we are absolutely certain concerning the promise and threat of God, this gives us comfort because we know that we have reached this station due the grace of God. If we have absolute faith in the obscure verses in the Qur'an and we depute their meanings to God this gives us relaxation. If we delve into the depths of obscure scriptural expressions, speculating as to their meanings with no firm proof as to the veracity of our speculation, we are tormented. Imam Tahawi explains this truth in the following words of his great treatise on the Muslim creed:

> Whoever covets knowledge that was barred from him, discontented with the limits of his understanding, shall be veiled from pure unity, unadulterated comprehension, and sound faith on account of his covetousness. He will then vacillate between belief and disbelief, assertion and negation, and resolution and denial. Obsessive, aimless, skeptical, and deviant, he is neither an assertive believer nor a resolute denier.[40]

Such empty speculation is the hallmark of skepticism. A skeptic despises a believer: He sees a believer as being smug and self-assured. The believer's state is the state of a refined human being. The skeptic is tormented and sees his state as embodying the true nature of the human condition—that we are essentially wretched in this world, condemned to a life, described in the words of the famous British philosopher, Thomas Hobbes, as "…solitary, poor, nasty, brutish, and short."⁴¹ This idea of the wretchedness of the human condition has grown up with skepticism. The Qur'anic worldview posits that with faith one can move away from the torment of doubt and skepticism into the comfort and delight of certainty, despite the trials and tribulations one has to deal with in this world.

That comfort comes through the remembrance of God. God couples His remembrance with peace of mind and tranquility of heart in the Qur'an. He says, *Those who believe and their hearts find tranquility in the remembrance of God. Surely, the remembrance of God brings tranquility to the hearts.* (13:28)

God, says, may His remembrance be venerated, *God is the protecting friend of those who believe, He brings them forth from darkness into light.* (2:257)

In the Qur'an, darkness is always mentioned in its plural form—*Dhulumat*. This emphasizes that the varieties of darkness are many. Among them we could mention, idolatry, disbelief, oppression, lying, cheating, fornication, stealing, doubt, pornography, gluttony, etc. Light is always mentioned in the singular—*Nur*. Truth is one for it emanates from the One, God, who is *al-Haqq* (the Truth). Involvement with any one of the varieties of darkness will inevitably open the door to involvement with others. A person trapped in such a state will be torn and unfocused in his of her life. When one basks in the light of faith, one will find that God focuses one's concerns and worldly involvements, and makes them subservient to a single concern, seeking His good pleasure.

Rather, those who can discern this and long to attain [these states] are people possessing sound intellect and an understanding of God. They work to implement the clear unambiguous rulings and avoid doubtful issues. The Prophet mentioned, "The lawful is clear and the unlawful is clear and between them are doubtful matters."[42]

People possessing clarity in their religious life do not try to interpret, avoid or create confusion around things that are clear. They implement them with faith and fidelity, confident in the reward they have been promised by God. The religious guidance we need to ensure our salvation is clear, in terms of what we need to know of the commandments and prohibitions of God. Between those clear commandments and prohibitions are doubtful matters, which should be avoided because we do not know what the consequences of delving into them would be.

Let us present you with a parable. We have three containers before us. In one of them is some honey. It has the picture of a bee on its label. It appears thick and viscous and its color is a rich golden brown. It is very sweet to the taste and we feel invigorated and uplifted after we drink it. This is clearly lawful and beneficial. In another container is a suspicious looking substance with a very foul odor. Its label contains the image of a skull and cross-bones, and the word "poison" is written on it. In its immediate vicinity are several dead insects. This is clearly something harmful to be avoided.

In a third container we have something that looks like honey but it has a skull and cross-bones on its label along with the word "poison." It does not have a foul odor, nor are their any dead insects in its immediate vicinity. Should we consider it honey and drink it, or should we consider it poison and avoid it? We are doubtful concerning it. If we avoid it we are spared its potential harm. Furthermore, we already have honey in the first container. If we consume it, it could well be poison and it will kill us. Therefore, it is far better for us to avoid it. This is how we should approach our religion. We should leave doubtful matters, because they can lead to a bad and undesired consequence, despite their sometimes harmless appearance.

"Leaving them is better then delving into them."

To extend the previous parable, we drink from the third vessel containing the doubtful substance. Nothing happens. However, do we know what will happen the next time in a similar situation? Over time, we lose respect for the skull and cross-bones. Sooner or later, due our lack of caution, we consume something poisonous and die.

Similarly, the person who engages in doubtful matters loses respect for forbidden things (*Haram*). Like the negligent shepherd, he grazes around the sanctuary of the king, almost entering it. He becomes accustomed to being around its perimeter and thinks there are no guards around, so he eventually sends his sheep into the forbidden pasturage. Suddenly, guards descend from the trees; slaughtering all of the sheep which have intruded into the sanctuary of the king, and possibly taking the life of the shepherd also.

Examine your intention.

Why would anyone want to engage in a doubtful matter? What is his intention (*niyya*), especially when he already has the equivalent of honey in his religious life? He already has something which is beneficial, what more does he need? Does he desire to be the only one who has said something profound about a verse of ambiguous import? He will find that the intention surrounding delving into an obscure matter will always be negative. Surely, God knows best.

Know your objective. Verily, recompense is based on intention. The Prophet said, "Actions are judged by their intentions and every person will have what he intended."[43]

If we intend to draw near to God by lawful means and by implementing the lawful and by avoiding the prohibited then we make a sincere intention to do just that and we will find that it suffices us. As we mentioned above, our intention for engaging in doubtful matters can only be related to building ourselves up or removing ourselves from the path of our righteous forbears. If we are able to give an unprecedented explanation of a particular text of ambiguous import, this is something that distinguishes us. When we see ourselves moving in that direction we need to quickly examine our intentions.

Be ever mindful of the commandments and prohibitions of God. The Muslim is "one who keeps other Muslims safe from his hand and his tongue, and the believer is the one who keeps all people safe from his wickedness."

Mindfulness of God or God-consciousness (*Taqwa*) is one of the foundational principles of our religion. *Taqwa* is more than mere consciousness of God, as it involves actions—specifically implementing His commandments and avoiding those things He has prohibited. Such actions are the essence of piety. However, it involves more than piety as those actions emanate from our consciousness of God.

Taqwa, from one perspective, involves three levels. A level that is relevant for all Muslims, which includes what we have just mentioned. Namely, implementing the orders and avoiding the prohibitions. A second level is relevant for those who have made a conscious effort to travel the spiritual path and endeavor to attain successively higher levels of spiritual refinement. This level involves consistently implementing those things that are encouraged by the divine law and avoiding those things that are discouraged. A final level is relevant for those who have reached the end of the spiritual path. It involves leaving off indulgence in permissible things when it is feared that they may take valuable time that could be devoted to involvement in obligatory or desirable things, or when it is feared that their overindulgence may lead to impermissible or disliked things.

Here, the Muslim is defined as a person who does not harm or abuse his or her fellow Muslim. This is a state we should all commit ourselves to upholding. Unfortunately, there are Muslims who have dedicated their careers to slandering, vilifying, and disparaging other Muslims. May God protect us from such actions.

The believer, in this context is at a higher level of faith than the Muslim. Therefore, his benefit is deeper and more comprehensive. He keeps all people, whether they are Muslims or others, safe from any harm, whether that involves the harm of his tongue and hands, or other things.

We should know that we can also harm ourselves. So we should make sure that we are safe from ourselves. We know from the Qur'an that there is a category of people who are described as those who oppress themselves (*dhalimun li Nafsihi*) (35:32). When we delve into doubtful matters we are oppressing ourselves, because we are wasting valuable time that we could have used to do something beneficial for our souls. Our exploration of such matters is a meaningless pursuit that involves no tangible or beneficial consequences.

To return to the theme of the Muslim sparing his coreligionists his harm, if you are a Muslim, ask yourself, "Are other people safe from my tongue and hands?" "Are they safe from any harm initiated by me?" If they are not, we can be assured that the teachings of Islam have not penetrated our hearts despite the outward appearances of faith that may accompany us. It is a sad situation when we find a person who looks pious, wears a turban or a headscarf, but engages in backbiting, slander, and accuses people of various indiscretions. Where is his faith?

Abu Bakr said, "Be mindful of God by obeying Him, and obey God by being mindful of Him. Restrain your hand that it never sheds the blood of a Muslim, restrain your stomach that it never consumes their wealth, and restrain your tongue that it is never defiled by transgressing against their honor."

We should make a covenant with God that we will never shed the blood of a Muslim, unless it is for a lawful reason. We should pray to God to protect us from ever allowing our hands to be stained with the blood of a Muslim, even if he has transgressed against us. We should never allow our tongue to be defiled by eating the flesh of a Muslim by backbiting him, or even worse, by slandering him. In this section the author is making a point that is specifically germane to Muslims. Hence, we see his emphasis on upholding the sanctity of a Muslim's life. However, the point he is making here is relevant for all innocent lives—both Muslims and members of other faith communities.

The literal meaning of this sentence is a warning against cheating, usurping, exploiting or otherwise taking a Muslim's wealth unlawfully, and then using that money to feed oneself.

However, it also means using ill-begotten wealth in any way, or gaining it via any scheme. One of these ways is by giving false testimony against a person in order to take his or her wealth. Such a testimony is referred to as the "immersing oath" (al-Yamin al-Ghamus). It is so called because the right hand that is raised to affirm a false testimony before a judge is the same hand that will one day immerse the perpetrator into the depths of Hell.

At the end of the hadith that mentions one of the foundations of Muslim brotherhood. The Prophet, peace upon him, mentions, "Every Muslim is sacred to his fellow Muslim—his life, his possessions and his honor."[44] God has placed the Muslim in a sanctuary. It is a sanctuary that provides for his or her protection. To encroach into that sanctuary is a grave offense that involves severe consequences. In these days when we see that in some places Muslims are literally at war with their coreligionists, we should be especially diligent in avoiding the matters Imam al-Muhasibi is warning us against.

Take yourself to account for every thought.

Every time we do something significant we should step back and assess it. Was it right? Was it lawful? Should I have done it? Such an accounting is a process that elevates us. On the other hand, if we fail to take an account of our actions we can easily enter upon a slippery slope that culminates in profligacy. Entry upon that slope begins with small things.

Something that is potentially ruinous to us begins as a thought. If we do not cut off that thought at some point, it becomes a habit, and when it becomes a habit, it becomes extremely difficult to get rid of. So we are reminded to stop it at the very beginning of its "lifecycle" by remembering God, before it gains control over us.

Imam al-Muhasibi is setting a very high standard for us by suggesting that our accounting should move beyond our actions, it should also include our very thoughts. We should remember that his impeccability in taking himself to account led to his nickname, "al-Muhasibi," which means one who takes an intense accounting of himself.

Be mindful that God is watching over you with every breath that you take.

As Ibn 'Ata Allah says in his *Aphorisms*, "There is no breath that you take except that there is an attendant ordainment that has been issued by God."[45] So we should try to take account for all of our breathes, meaning we should monitor our time to insure that we neither waste it in idle pursuits, or allow something negative to occur during the time of that breathe due to our negligence.

We should also endeavor to understand what God's ruling is for the time that a particular breathe occurs in. In other words, we should try to understand what we should be doing during every moment of our lives. This is what it means when we say that the Sufi is the child of the moment (*ibn al-Waqt*). He endeavors to live a life consistent with God's plan. Insight into that plan, as it unfolds in our life, can be gained if we contemplate the direction God is leading us towards. This understanding, once attained, helps us to avoid wasting time and energy in the pursuit of those things God is not facilitating for us.

'Umar mentioned, "Take yourself to account before you are taken to account, weigh your actions before they are weighed,[46] and beautify yourself for the ultimate presentation.[47] On that day not the slightest secret will be hidden."

When we take ourselves to account, there is time to change. We have time to step back from negative actions and to increase our good actions. When we are taken to account, it is too late and there is no time to change anything. Hence, we should take the advice offered us by 'Umar, and try to take a regular accounting of our actions.

If we see that we are falling short and engaging in a lot of negativity, and we find that our good deeds are scant, then this is an indication that we might come up short when our account is taken by God. If we find this to be the case, then we must immediately begin heaping more good deeds into our scale. This is done by engaging in more righteous acts in all of their manifestations, and ensuring that we are not adding bad deeds to our record.

How will we appear when we are presented before God? Ask yourself this question, for we will eventually stand before Him. If we engaged in a life of wicked deeds and slander, we will stand before God in an ugly and pathetic state. We will be full of shame and remorse. On the other hand, if we have lived a life working righteous deeds and have adorned ourselves and beautified ourselves with piety, then we will stand before Him as proud and dutiful employees stand before a just and generous employer. We should adorn ourselves with piety and righteous deeds to prepare ourselves to stand before God in a beautiful way. This is one of the things that we should never lose focus on in this world.

If we truly fear God in our religion, we will fear God in our worldly affairs. This truism arises from the fact that our religion encompasses our worldly affair. How we behave in conducting our worldly business should not be divorced from our religious life. Our work and our play should be an articulation of our religious beliefs and ethics. Hence, if our religion is in order, our worldly affairs should be in order.

This understanding is relevant to what Imam al-Muhasibi mentions here. Nothing we do in this world, whether we consider it a religious or worldly endeavor, escapes God. There is no realm of action that is hidden from God. Sadly, we see many Muslims who are extremely careful in performing actions that they believe to be strictly religious, such as praying and fasting. However, in their pursuit of their livelihood there are many Muslims who lack any scruples. An example of such people is one who is in the first row of every prayer. He never misses the Morning Prayer in congregation, yet he will sell alcohol, pork and pornography in his shop. It is as if he believes that God's observance of him stops once he leaves the mosque.

Fear God in your religion, and hope for good from God in all of your affairs.

Make the ultimate objective of everything you do a quest for the Pleasure of God, and a means of facilitating meeting God in a good state. The Prophet, peace upon him, mentioned: "Those who long for the meeting with God, God is pleased to meet them."[48] We should be people who long to meet God. How could it be otherwise when we realize how much God has done for us, and when we reflect on the vastness of His blessings, and the preponderance of His grace? Even a person who has suffered greatly in this world has been blessed. He has been blessed with this life that opens up for him the possibility of eternal bliss in Paradise. Exposure to that bliss for even a moment will make him forget all of the ill he suffered in the world.[49]

Patiently endure whatever afflicts you.

We are going to be afflicted, to greater or lesser extents, in this world. The nature of the world is that it is the abode of trials, tribulations, and afflictions. God, Most High, tells us this emphatically in the Qur'an, *Surely you will be tested with some degree of fear, hunger and loss of wealth, lives and fruits. Give glad tidings to those who patiently persevere. Those who when afflicted by a tragedy say, "We belong to God and unto Him we are all returning."* (2:156) Patience, as we are taught, is one of the greatest virtues. Sufficient for the Muslim, in terms of understanding its virtue, is the magnitude of its reward. God mentions in this regard, *Rather, the patient ones will be given their recompense with no numerical limitations.* (39:10)

We should understand that patience is the counsel of those exempted from ruin. God says, *By the witness of time through the ages, surely humankind is lost, except those who believe and do righteous deeds. They counsel each other with truth; and they counsel each other with patience.* (103:1-3)

Imam 'Ali said, "Do not fear anything except your sins. Do not long for anything other than your Lord. Let no one of you lacking knowledge be too shy to ask until he learns. Do not let one who is asked something he lacks knowledge of refrain from saying, 'I do not know.'"

What will eventually ruin us? Our sins! Satan will not ruin us, nor will people, nor will the vicissitudes of time. At the end of the day, sin will be the cause of our ruin. Satan, people, the world and the vicissitudes of time are only callers who sometimes invite us to sin. We limit their potentially negative influence over us by being constant in the remembrance of God, and by keeping them in their proper place.

Who will ultimately save us? God! Ultimately there is no strength or power, no source of salvation or damnation, no source of any harm or benefit except God. Therefore, we should stop running away from Him and we should begin running towards Him. We are urged in the Qur'an, *Flee to God! Verily I am from Him unto you a clear warner.* (51:50)

How do we obtain the knowledge of our religion? We obtain it by asking others. Mujahid, who was one of the great Qur'an commentators from the second generation of Muslims, said, "The shy one and the arrogant one will never attain knowledge." Why? Because the shy one is prevented by his of her shyness from asking, and the arrogant one thinks he already knows everything. He is usually described as one afflicted by compound ignorance. He does not know and he is too ignorant to even realize that he does not know.

One of the great virtues of the early generations of Muslims was that they would not be too shy or arrogant to seek knowledge of the issues they were ignorant concerning. If they found no means to address their ignorance they would respond to an inquiry by simply saying, "I do not know." Imam al-Mawardi, one of the great scholars of the Muslims, relates a story where he was forced to concede he did know the answers to a series of questions put to him by two desert Arabs.[50] He relates that Ibn 'Abbas said, "If a scholar stops saying, 'I do not know,' he has met his fatal affliction."[51] A scholar mentioned, "One who stops saying, 'I do not know,' is ruined."[52]

The willingness of people possessing true knowledge to readily admit their ignorance arises from their desire not to speak about issues related to God's religion without possessing sure knowledge. They know that speaking without knowledge is a grave sin. It has been related that the Prophet, peace upon him, said, "Whoever is given a baseless answer to a question; the sin is on the one who answered him."[53]

These and similar narrations illustrate the humility that is essential for a real scholar. Knowledge is a gift from God that He gives to those who are humble, pious, and whose hearts are detached from the trappings of this world. Someone might mention that he knows a scholar who is arrogant. If he knows of such a person he should understand that in that scholar's case knowledge is not a gift. Rather, it is a tribulation from God that will lead that person to his ruin.

You should know that the relationship between patience and faith is like the relationship between the head and the body.

If you have no patience, your faith will eventually be eroded. Patience is the ingredient that allows faith to produce its fruits. Actions cannot be consistent if the person initiating them, from the point of view of human initiative, lacks patience. When actions lack consistency the benefit they provide to one undertaking them will be limited. Hence, the most beloved of all acts with God are those done most consistently even if they appear to be small in and of themselves. The Prophet, peace upon him, mentioned in this regard to 'Abdullah bin 'Amr bin al-'As, warning him against inconsistency in his actions, "Do not be like so-and-so. He used to perform the night prayer and then he left it.⁵⁴

When the head is cut-off, the entire body dies. Therefore, if you hear something that angers you or offends your honor, pardon the perpetrator and overlook the slight. That is firmness of purpose.

We are trying to move to God and that requires focus and patient determination. If we are constantly responding to the slights of people or to their petty insults, we will never be able to gather the energy necessary to make meaningful spiritual progress. Overlooking such distractions is one of the keys to spiritual elevation and it is a display of firmness and resolve in one's affair.

'Umar bin al-Khattab said, "One who fears God does not give vent his rage. He also refrains from doing whatever his ego desires. Were it not for the fact of the Day of Resurrection, you would see things totally different than they are now."

Increasingly we see a lack of moral restraint in this society. The system of taboos and prohibitions that formerly served to check people's actions has been systematically eroded. What is there to check people? In his book, *The Death of Satan,* Andrew Delbanco makes the point that people no longer fear God, nor Satan.[55] This situation leads to the loss of a common morality that is necessary for constructive social life. In the absence of a unifying moral code, human life degenerates into a jungle-like condition qualified by an ethos of "a war of all against all." The weak, downtrodden, oppressed, and marginalized are left to suffer according to the whims of the rich and powerful.

In the resulting atmosphere it becomes easy to lie, steal, cheat and kill. All of these are major national crises contemporarily. To begin to address these issues effectively, we have to work for a return of God-consciousness in our society, coupled with a healthy portion of fear and self-restraint. Returning to the path of decency and moral rectitude is always possible. However, it will never occur without belief in God. God mentions in the Qur'an, *Corruption has appeared on the land and sea because of what the hands of humans have wrought. This is in order that He (God) gives them a taste of what they have brought about, in order that they return.* (30:41)

In the concluding part of this passage, 'Umar is saying that if people did not fear that they were accountable to God in the Hereafter then his time would have witnessed the sorts of behavior we see today—vile actions that illustrate a total lack of moral restraint, while displaying no expectation of punishment in the hearts of those committing them. Most people do not think that there is a Day of Judgment and because of this there is no moral restraint. There is no patience. We seek instant gratification. This state of affairs is characterized by greed, vicious competition for material things, and an increasing disregard for the rights and property of others.

Therefore, guard your concerns.

What is our ultimate concern? It should be attaining Paradise and the Beatific Vision. We have to guard and protect this concern. This is something that takes tremendous effort and divine help. Therefore, the Prophet, peace upon him, taught us to pray, "O God! Do not make this world our greatest concern or the extent of our knowledge."[56]

One of the most profound Islamic teachings in this regard is found in the following hadith:

> Whoever makes the world his greatest concern, God will divide him between his various concerns, and make his poverty self-evident. Furthermore, he will only get from the world what has been determined for him. As for the one who makes the Hereafter his greatest concern, God gives him focus in his affairs, places his wealth in his heart, and the world will be subservient to him, even if he desires otherwise.[57]

Be preoccupied with addressing your faults from not seeking out the faults of others.

What this means is that you should avoid searching for negativity in other people. This does not mean that when you see things wrong you cannot or should not give sincere counsel in private. However, generally speaking, we should be preoccupied with first and foremost reforming ourselves, and not condemning others, while leaving our own shortcomings unaddressed. One of the greatest blessings God can give us is showing us our faults. When we know them we can correct them. To be blinded by our own faults and only seeing the faults of others is an indication that God is displeased with us. By pointing out the faults of others, to the exclusion of our own, our faults grow—unaddressed—until they ruin us.

CHAPTER TWO

It used to be said, "It is sufficient proof that a person's character is flawed that he finds in others the same faults he himself possesses, yet they are hidden from him; that he hates in people things he himself does; that he offends those sharing his company, or that he discusses other people's business when it is not his concern."

God says, addressing the believers in the strongest words of condemnation, *Grievously hated is it with God that you say what you do not do.* (61:3) He says, addressing the Rabbis, *Do you command people with righteousness and then refuse to do it yourself, and all the while you are reciting the scripture? Will you not reflect?* (2:44)

Islam is trying to make us people of integrity and lofty principles, far removed from hypocrisy and pettiness. One of the keys to attaining such a position is through consistent, truthful implementation of everything we preach or teach. The lessons of religion are all designed to be implemented not merely memorized or studied as part of an academic exercise. We should always be aware of the fact that not only do we hurt ourselves when we fail to practice what we preach we also help to undermine the integrity of the religion itself. We become the excuse some people will use to justify their own debauchery.

All of our gatherings should be qualified by dignity, safety, serenity, and mutual benefit. To harm someone sitting in your company is like slandering, vilifying, striking or otherwise abusing one's guest. The harm accruing to one who abuses those sitting in his company is warded off if we take the following advice to heart and implement its lessons. The Prophet, peace upon him, said:

> Whoever believes in God and the Last Day let him speak well or remain silent. Whoever believes in God and the Last Day let him honor his guest. And whoever believes in God and the Last Day let him honor his neighbor.[58]

It is mentioned in a well-known hadith, "From a person's Islam being good is his leaving what does not concern him."[59] If one's religious orientation is sound one is concerned about doing those things that will help one gain Paradise. Nothing else is our immediate concern. One of the things that do concern us is good treatment of the neighbor. In this case the neighbor includes anyone who shares our vicinity. That may be the inhabitants of a home close to ours or those sitting near us. They are all deserving of our good treatment.

Ibn Rajab said, concerning good Islam:

> When Islam is good it requires a person leave everything that does not concern him; be that matter forbidden, doubtful, disliked, or even excessive engagement in something permissible, when he does not need it. None of these things concern a Muslim

when his religion is complete and he reaches the level of inner excellence. If he fails to see Him (God), then he should know that He observes him. Therefore, one who worships God with an awareness of just how close He is to him and that He is indeed watching over him, such a person has made his religion good. This makes it necessary that he leaves what does not concern him.[60]

Use your intellect to worship God by not being obsessed with your plans.

Ibn 'Ata Allah mentions in his *Aphorisms*, "Relax from being obsessed with your plans; what someone else has undertaken on your behalf, do not burden yourself with it."[61] Some people view this and similar expressions to be articulations of a fatalistic worldview that has worked to stifle the material progress of Muslims. They point to such teachings as barriers between the Muslims and the attainment of a Calvinist work ethic. In their haste to ward off such accusations many Muslims respond, "No! We are Calvinists. The real dynamic Islam of the early generations of Muslims completely embodied the Calvinist work ethic." They then find "Calvinistic" scriptures to prove it. It is as if the object of Islam is to place us on a path that will result in us becoming a group of neurotic capitalists.

We should understand that this aphorism does not mean abandoning planning. 'Umar mentioned, "Half of [your] livelihood is good planning."[62] Everything in the Prophet's message and life emphasizes good planning. For example, when he migrated from Mecca to Medina, he developed an elaborate plan. He did not just set off for Medina, saying, "I trust in God, He will protect me." He planned. Medina is to the north of Mecca, but he left from the south. He left Imam

'Ali in his bed to buy time for himself and his companion. He had Abu Bakr's son cover up his tracks with his herd of goats. He took shelter in a cave. He took a guide with him. He took every means to facilitate his success. Then after all of that, he trusted in God concerning the outcome of those plans.

What the aphorism we quoted above means is that we should not be obsessed with the outcome of our plans to such an extent that when those plans do not turn out the way we desire we become upset and may even begin to doubt God's power and wisdom. Plan, organize, work, but trust in God concerning the outcomes.

Effective planning is a neglected aspect of the prophetic way. When the Prophet, peace upon him, arrived in Medina, he took a census: What skills did the people possess? How many Jews were in Medina? How many idolaters? What are the various power bases? Who were the influential notables of the city? How many men, women, children, workers, warriors were to be found?

After that he undertook a massive public health campaign. We read about it in isolated hadiths. For example, "Do not urinate in stagnant water."[63] "Do not leave the vessels uncovered in your houses overnight."[64] There had been an outbreak of malaria when the Prophet arrived in Medina. It had devastated the migrants from the dry climate of Mecca. The Prophet, peace upon him, ordered that the swamps around the city be drained to push the mosquitoes away from the populated areas.

The Prophet, peace upon him, just did not say, "God will make it better," he took steps to eliminate unhealthy situations that were breeding pests that carried various diseases. Hence, it was planning, organization, administration and management that allowed the fledgling community to establish a base in Medina. These are some of the things that made the Muslims successful. After doing these things they relied on God that the outcome would be positive.

Rely on God, that He will ward off from you [the harm] contained in the divine ordainment.

Supplication is the weapon of the believer. So pray to God. A great example of the power of prayer is found in the biography of Imam al-Shafi'i. When he was a judge in Yemen he refused to be corrupted. The governor, who was trying to get him to compromise his standards, accused him of being a Shiite conspirator involved in a plot to subvert the rule of Harun al-Rashid in Yemen. He informed al-Rashid of the alleged "conspiracy" and al-Rashid ordered Imam al-Shafi'i and a group of coconspirators extradited from Yemen to Baghdad.

All of the others were executed. When it was the turn of Imam al-Shafi'i he made a prayer, "O God! You are the most gentle in dealing with your servants. I ask your gentleness as the divine ordainment [unfolds in my life]." After making this prayer, he entered into a dialogue with the Caliph who realized that this was a person of incredible learning and knowledge, a man far elevated above the base charges that had been levied against him. Hence, Imam al-Shafi'i was saved.[65]

Imam 'Ali said, "O son of Adam, do not delight in wealth, and do not be overwhelmed with grief when you are afflicted with poverty. Do not be saddened by tribulations."

Wealth is a blessing and a test. It allows us to give charity, to support good causes and to assist others. However, it also lengthens our reckoning, increases our responsibilities before God, and invites envy. Poverty can be a blessing, as well a great test. It makes our reckoning lighter, it turns others away from us, and it gives us more time to worship God. So do not be overwhelmed when tested with poverty. Patiently persevere, enjoy the opportunity to worship God more intensely, and trust that God will bring you relief.

Trials and tribulations can be indicators of God's love. The Prophet, peace upon him, mentioned, "If God loves a people He tests them."[66] People are also tested to the extent of their faith. The Prophet, peace upon him, was asked, "Which people are most severely tested?" He replied, "The Prophets, peace upon them, and then on down from them. A man is tested according to his faith."[67] Thus, trials and tribulations are a sign of faith, and an indication that one has a good standing with God. Furthermore, we should understand that God does not place on anyone a burden greater than they can bear. So if you are tested by God, bear that test with patience and dignity. If you are able to do so you will witness tremendous spiritual gifts and unimaginable benefits.

Ibn 'Ata Allah reminds us that tests are a gift from God that He uses to familiarize Himself to us.[68] They provide us with an opportunity to get to know the reality of His names and attributes. He is the Compeller who is capable of incapacitating us at a time we are enjoying good health. He is the Healer who alone is capable of restoring our health, or bringing us relief from those things that vex or oppress us. If trials, tribulations, disease or afflictions involve circumstances that allow us to gain a deeper understanding of God, then they are gifts from Him whose acceptance brings us nearer to Him in ways our actions never could.

This world, as God repeatedly informs us in the Qur'an, is the abode of trials and tribulations. God says, *He has created death and life in order to test you; which of you are best in deed. He is overwhelmingly mighty, oft-forgiving.*" (67:2) He also says, *We will surely test you with something of fear, hunger, and loss of wealth, life and fruits. Give glad tidings to those who patiently persevere.*

(2:155) Similarly, *Do people think that they will be left alone to simply allege, 'We believe!' and then not be tested? We have tested those who preceded them in order that God will show which of them are truthful and which of them are liars.* (29:2) All of these verses emphasize that this world is an abode of tests. The object of life is not to avoid or deny its tests and trials, rather to successfully pass them.

Another verse forthrightly presents a fact alluded to in the above-citations. Namely, the tests in this world will involve what we refer to as good, and what we refer to as evil. God says in that regard, *Every soul will experience death, and we will test you with evil and good, as a trial; and unto us you will return.* (21:35) This verse makes it clear that God has never promised us a rose garden in this worldly life. Muslims were never promised that we would win every battle.[69] We were never promised that our "Ummah" would march triumphantly through history, in Hegelian or Darwinian fashion, leaving inferior systems of belief, and social organization strewn in our wake. We were certainly never promised that, through science, we would be able to conquer the forces of nature, which have always hung menacingly over the head of humanity.[70]

The great sage, Ibn 'Ata Allah Sakandari, beautifully captured the reality of this world, and what our expectations in it should be, when he said:

> Do not find the occurrence of tribulations strange as long as you are in this worldly abode, for it has only manifested its deserved description, its intrinsic characteristic.[71]

Living in this world will inevitably bring us tests. Those tests are subtle and open, they occur in great and small things. Through these tests, God shows those of us who truly believe, and those who are empty claimants.[72]

Many think that tests from God are always signs of His wrath. As Muslims, we believe that the trials afflicting us can be signs of His Love. God's Messenger, peace upon him, informed us:

> The magnitude of otherworldly reward is proportionate to the magnitude of worldly tribulation. When God loves a people, He tries them. Whoever is content, will have divine pleasure. Whoever is displeased will have divine wrath.[73]

As the Prophets, peace upon them, are the most beloved of humanity with God, it follows that their tribulations should be greater than those of ordinary folks. This is indeed the case. In this regard, as a hadith we have mentioned earlier in this section bears out, no one was more severely tested than the Messenger of God, Muhammad, peace upon him. He lost his father before his birth, he lost his mother during his infancy, his male children all died, he was forced to emigrate from his home, his Companions were killed and forced into exile, he was boycotted and humiliated, his beloved wife died at a critical juncture in his mission, and he faced many other trials and tribulations. 'Aisha reported, "I never saw anyone more tested with pain than the Messenger of God, peace upon him."[74]

Do not be overly pleased by easy times. Verily, gold is tested for its purity by fire. Likewise, a righteous servant is tested by tribulations.

During easy times we should intensify our worship. We should try to get close to God. By worshipping intensely during the easy times, we "familiarize" ourselves to God. The scholars say that one of the results of a person constantly worshipping God in easy circumstances is that God becomes accustomed to hearing that person's voice. Therefore, when he calls on him during difficult times, God hears him and He responds. The Prophet, peace upon him, mentioned, "Get to know God during the easy times. He will know you during the hard times."[75]

Gold is purified by fire in a process referred to as *Tamhis*. God mentions this term in the Qur'an when He discusses how He will test the believers ...*so that God can purify the ranks of the Believers.*" (3:141) God mentions this *Tamhis* in the trial of the believer as indispensable for selecting the people who will take the religion forward. The fire that God tests the believers with is the fire of trials, tribulation, and disease. If we patiently persevere through whatever God chooses to test us with, we will emerge from those tests purified. It is related in a sound hadith, "When I test my believing servant and He does not levy a complaint against Me to those visiting him, I will release him from the restraints on My servants, and then substitute for him flesh better than his flesh, and blood better than his blood. Thereafter, let him resume his actions."[76]

You will never attain what you desire except by leaving off what you have a strong craving for.

We will not get to God without leaving something of this world. God says, *You will never attain righteousness until you spend from that which you love.* (3:92) So the key to righteousness is to spend—money, possessions, desires, clothing, habits, anything that we long for and is dear to us. This conditions us to keep the world and all of its possessions in perspective. In our system of spiritual purification, our adornment with the lofty characteristics of faith is always preceded by the cleansing or removal of old, undesirable qualities, actions, or characteristics. We read in the Qur'an, *Whoever rejects the false god and then believes in God has grasped a firm handhold that will never break.* (2:256)

You will not reach the level you anticipate except through persevering with what is displeasing to you.

One of the poets said:

I will consider every difficulty easy, until I obtain my aspirations. Desires are only made subservient to those who patiently persevere.[77]

God only elevates those who exert themselves. Any thing of value in this world has to be worked for, and there is nothing more valuable than a purified soul and a rectified heart. Concerning the latter, God mentions in the Qur'an, *A day when neither wealth nor children will be of any benefit, except for one coming before God with a rectified heart.* (26:88-89)

In the spiritual path, one of the most beneficial forms of exertion is in opposing the whims of one's soul. One of the sages mentioned, "Opposing the whims of your soul is the essence of your cure." This saying is consistent with the message of the Qur'anic verse, *As for the one who fears the station of his Lord and guards his soul against its whims, Paradise will be his repose.*(79:40) This is one of the fundamental lessons of the spiritual path. One who fails to heed it will not make any real progress towards his or her Lord.

Exert your utmost in guarding the obligations God has made incumbent upon you.

Again, this is one of the foundations of the spiritual path. One who does not carefully guard and diligently perform the obligations God has established will find the door leading to the spiritual path closed in his or her face. No one enters upon the path except through the door of sincere faith and fulfilling the binding obligations. God mentions in a divine hadith, "No one draws himself close to Me with anything more beloved to Me than the obligations I have imposed on him..."[78]

By guarding our obligations we find that we are protected by God. The Prophet, peace upon him, advised one of his young Companions, "Guard the obligations imposed by God and He will protect you."[79] That protection includes the protection from Hell by facilitating the performance of those acts that ward off from us punishment in the Hereafter.

Be pleased with what God has desired for you. Ibn Mas'ud said, "Be pleased with what God has measured out for you and you will be the wealthiest of people. Avoid what God has forbidden for you and you will be the most impeccable of people. Perform the obligatory acts God, Most High, has imposed upon you and you will be the most devout of people."

Ibn Mas'ud said, "Be pleased with what God has proportioned out for you and you will be the wealthiest of people." Pleasure with the Ordainment of God is one of the greatest guarantors of security and happiness. Wealth and poverty, by Islamic standards, has nothing to do with material possessions, it is based on contentment and discontent. If you are content with what you have been blessed with, you are wealthy. This is because wealth is not the possession of abundance, wealth is freedom from need.

We say that God is *al-Ghani*, because He is free from all needs. He is also, *al-Hamid*, worthy of all praise. We read in the Qur'an, *O people! You are in desperate need of God. As for God, He is free of all needs, worthy of all praise.* (35:15) Hence, if you possess very little and do not need any more, you are wealthy. On the other hand, if you possess much, but you are unsatisfied and need an increase, you are impoverished.

One of the greatest manifestations of our freedom from need, and hence our wealth, is not needing to engage in forbidden things. We are not tempted by them because we have absolutely no need for them. This is one of the fruits of sound faith. To reiterate the prophetic hadith, "From a person's Islam being good is his leaving what does not concern him."[80] Hence, his ability to leave prohibited things, which are definitely not his concern, is one of the surest indications of sound religion. It is also an indication of God's grace in the life of a servant.

Taqwa as we have mentioned earlier, is sometimes translated as "God-consciousness," and sometimes it is rendered, "piety." In reality, it is a combination of both. It is a degree of God-consciousness that manifests itself in piety. Piety in turn lies in avoiding those things that God has forbidden and doing those things He has commanded.

Devotion is closely associated with piety. The difference between the two lies in the fact that devotion speaks more of our motivation for undertaking our actions. Devotion can arise from many different sources such as seeking God's reward or good pleasure, fleeing from his punishment, out of thankfulness to Him, or simply as an expression of our love.

Ibn Juzayy al-Kalbi mentions ten ascending motivations that push believers towards righteous actions:

1.   Fear of an otherworldly punishment.
2.   Fear of a worldly punishment.
3.   Hope for a worldly reward.
4.   Hope for an otherworldly reward.
5.   Fear of a [difficult] reckoning.
6.   Shyness before God's all-encompassing gaze.

7. Thankfulness for His blessings with obedience.
8. Acknowledging His ontological uniqueness.
9. Magnifying the majesty of God.
10. The truthfulness of one's love for Him.[81]

We should always endeavor to move to a higher motivation until we readily implement all of His commandments and prohibitions based on the depth of our love for Him.

Do not complain against one who is most merciful to you, to one who is merciless towards you.

Do not complain about God to the creatures of God. God is merciful and everything He does for us, in open and hidden ways, is a manifestation of His mercy. He desires good for us. He is pleased with our salvation. He states in the Qur'an, *Rather, God has made faith beloved to you and adorned with it your hearts. And He has made you hate disbelief, corruption and sin.* (49:7)

Ultimately, God wants good for us, but we have to do our part. We have to be patient and let His ordainment unfold in our lives. When we are patient, we are blessed to see that in many instances what we may initially hastily believe to be something undesirable, turns out to be something of tremendous benefit. God's wisdom is deep, but if we are not patient we fail to perceive it owing to the shallowness of our wisdom.

In many instances, it is either our lack of patience or our failure to see God's wisdom that leads us to complain against Him to His creatures. As we grow and mature spiritually, hopefully we will be spared from falling into this behavior, which constitutes a tremendous breach of etiquette in terms of how we should relate to God.

Rely upon God, and you will be amongst the elite. 'Ubada bin al-Samit said to his son, "O My son! Despair of the idea that people can help you in any way, for this is true wealth. Beware of craving [people's possessions] and seeking their help to meet your needs, for this is true poverty."

Everything ultimately comes from God. The Prophet, peace upon him, said, "If you place your trust in anyone, place it in God. And if you ask for anything, ask it of God."[82]

God is most quick to help us. Sometimes He withholds from us what we ask of Him and that is the best help we could receive. However, oftentimes we fail to realize this. Reliance on God is one of the greatest practical expressions of real belief, for its essence lies in being surer of the bounty and grace possessed by God than we are in our own personal resources. For the believer, reliance on God is sufficient. God says in the Qur'an, *Whoever places his reliance on God, He will suffice him.* (65:3)

Imam Ahmad said that the happiest of his days was when he woke up and found nothing in his cabinets. That was a day he had to rely totally upon God.[83] We foster conditions, which work to remove our reliance on God. We save and horde money for a "rainy" day. We take out insurance policies to ward off the consequences of an unforeseen event. The cell phone helps to eliminate the "ghayb" of this world because we can instantaneously find out where someone is or what they are doing. Global communications and transportation networks bring our food from the far corners of the earth so we do not have to rely on God to bring the rains that will irrigate our local crops.

The cognitive frames that allow us to deal with religious belief are rooted in our experience. When our everyday experiences do not reinforce fundamental religious lessons and concepts, we have to work extra hard to enliven those meanings in our hearts.

One thing we can all do under our current circumstances is to realize that all of the people who are involved in bringing us the many benefits we enjoy can only do so because God has made them subservient to us. This will help us to be more aware of God's bounty and grace even in circumstances that tend to mitigate the ways we directly experience the manifestations of God's names and attributes in the world.

When you pray, let it be the prayer of one bidding farewell.

We should try to depart from the world in the very best of states. Each time we pray, we should think to ourselves that this could be our last prayer. Therefore, it could well be the last gift that we will present to God from this world. Will it be precious and priceless, or will it be base and cheap?

Our Prophet, peace upon him, warned us to guard our final actions.[84] That being the case we should be ever vigilant in our devotions because we never know which deed may be our last. Hence, all of our worship should be undertaken in the very best fashion. "God is beautiful and He loves beauty."[85] We should try to ensure that everything we present to God is beautiful. Anything less is unbefitting Him.

Know that you will not experience the sweetness of faith until you believe in the Ordainment of God— its good and evil.

Everything is from God. Nothing escapes His knowledge, will and ordainment. Of those things that unfold in the world are what we perceive to be good and what we perceive to be evil. However, as believers, we should try to look beyond perceptions. For us there is only good. The Prophet, peace upon him, relates in that regard, "Truly amazing is the affair of the believer, his affair only involves good. If he experiences good he thanks God, and that is best for him. And if he experiences a trial or tribulation he patiently endures it, and that is best for him. This state is only for the believer."[86]

As for the details relating to how the divine ordainment works as it interfaces with human initiative and free will, people can only speculate concerning that. That process involves a divine secret that God has not revealed to any of his servants. Much has been written in this area, by philosophers, theologians, mystics and others. However, none of their words are definitive. At the end of the day, such issues are unknown to us. We do know that God wants good for us and our task in this world is to wholeheartedly pursue that good.

Speak the truth and act on it, God will increase you in light and heart-vision.

Many times we readily perceive the superficial meanings of things, but miss their deeper, underlying meanings. Oftentimes, that is because we do not submit to God's wisdom. Therefore, we do not worship Him with unstinting devotion. We find that a lack of pure devotion often occurs due to our preoccupation with our worldly pursuits. God has guaranteed for us what we will take from this world. That being the case, we should not be led to believe that if we concentrate on our worldly affairs, and allow our striving for the Hereafter to suffer, somehow we will increase our preordained portion of worldly things.

This state of affairs only leads to the lessening of the light of our hearts, and, therefore, the weakening of our "heart-vision." The great sage and scholar, Ibn 'Ata Allah mentions in one of his aphorisms, "Your assiduous striving for what has been guaranteed for you, and you falling short in what has been demanded of you, is an indication that your heart-vision has been extinguished."[87] It is on the basis of this "heart-vision" that we come to understand the underlying meanings of things, and this vision is only as strong as the inner light that makes it possible.

Do not be like one who commands the truth, yet he is far from it, you are then forced to confess your sins, and are exposed to the anger of God. God says, *Grievously hated is it with God that you say what you do not do.* (61:3) The Messenger of God, peace upon him, said, "One who gives advice but is not admonished himself; who pulls other people back from ruination but he himself is not pulled back; and who forbids wrong, but he fails to heed his own admonition will be disappointed when he meets God."[88]

This warning is general. Every believer is enjoined to act upon what he or she knows. However, the warning is graver for the scholars who fail to act on their knowledge, or to heed their own counsel. Imam Ramli mentions in his didactic poem, *Safwa al-Zubad*:

The scholar who fails to act on the things he knows…
    will be taken to task before idolaters.[89]

Islam is a religion of action not talking. We are enjoined to implement whatever we know and not just talk about it. This is especially relevant for the scholars. Scholars are the heirs of the Prophets, peace upon them. The Prophets, peace upon them, left a legacy rooted in action. The scholars have been entrusted with that legacy. Any scholar failing to act to preserve it has behaved irresponsibly.

Only keep the company of intelligent, God-fearing people. Only sit in the presence of insightful, scholarly people.

The company we keep is critical for our spiritual journey. If we keep good company it will be a positive help to us and if we keep bad company that will affect us negatively. God has commanded us, *O believers! Be conscious of God and keep yourself in the company of the truthful.* (9:119) The Prophet, peace upon him, mentioned, "A person is on the religion of his companion. Therefore, let every one of you carefully consider the company he keeps."[90]

Merely sitting in the company of the righteous has its benefits. Hearts are affected by the energy of those hearts they come into contact with. People of a high spiritual state can affect you positively with their mere gaze. We should be mindful of these facts and carefully guard who and what we expose our hearts to.

The Prophet, peace upon him, was asked, "Which of our companions are best?" He said, "One whose appearance reminds you of the God, and whose speech increases you in knowledge, and whose actions remind you of the hereafter."

When the Prophet, peace upon him, entered Medina, one of the Jewish Rabbis exclaimed, upon gazing at him, "His face is not the face of a liar!"[91] We should try to increase our inner light so that we are able to both educate and elevate people without words. The best teacher is one who educates by means of his glance. When such people do speak, their speech is an increase in benefit and service. The Prophet, peace upon him, has said, as we have previously mentioned, "Whoever believes in God and the Last Day let him speak well or remain silent."[92]

True religion shines through a believer's face and impresses itself on others without words. It is subsequently manifested in uplifting and beneficial words. Try your best to find people of true religion and keep their company. Cherish the moments you can spend in their presence. "They are people that will never be a source of grief for those keeping their company."[93]

Humble yourself before the truth and make yourself subservient unto it.

When truth comes, all arguments should cease. A true argument is only a systematic effort to present or ascertain the truth. God mentions in the Qur'an that *Truth comes and falsehood perishes. Falsehood will inevitably perish.* (17:81) Humility is not just relevant for our actions. We should also learn to humble ourselves before the truth and to humble our opinions. In many instances, this is even more important than humility in our actions, owing to the import and gravity of our speech. We should always be mindful in this regard that no matter how hard we try to elevate ourselves, our ability to do so is limited. True elevation only comes from God, and his capabilities are unlimited. The Prophet, peace upon him, said, "No one humbles himself for the sake of God except that God elevates him."[94]

Constantly remember God and you will obtain nearness to Him.

Imam Ibn Qayyim al-Jawziyya mentions over one hundred benefits of God's remembrance in his book, *Al-Wabil al-Sayyib* (The Copious Downpour). We will mention a few of them. He says:

1. It repulses, represses and breaks the resolve of Satan.
2. It pleases the Most Merciful.
3. It removes concern and gloom from the heart.
4. It brings joy, happiness and delight to the heart.
5. It strengthens the heart and the body.
6. It illuminates the face and the heart.
7. It attracts sustenance.
8. It envelopes the remembering servant in reverence, sweetness and radiance.
9. It engenders love, which is the very spirit of Islam.
10. It brings awareness of God's surveillance.
11. It encourages repentance.
12. It brings nearness to God.
13. It opens one of the great doors of gnosis.
14. It brings about reverence, and veneration of his Lord.
15. It is coupled with God's remembrance of His remembering servant, as the Most High states, *Remember Me and I will remember you.* (2:152)[95]

In another one of his compilations, *Zad al-Ma'ad*, Imam Ibn Qayyim mentions the state of the Prophet, peace upon him, as it relates to his remembrance of God:

The Prophet, peace upon him, was the most perfect of creation in his remembrance of God. All of his speech involved God's remembrance. His commandments, prohibitions, and his legislating for his community were all forms of remembrance of God. [...] His thanking Him for His blessings and graces, his glorifying Him, his enumerating His praises were all forms of God's remembrance. His invocation, his supplication, his longing for the divine and his reverent fear of Him were all remembrance of God. His silent and tranquil moments were filled with the remembrance of God in his heart. His remembrance of God encompassed all of his states at all times. His remembrance of God flowed with every breath—standing, sitting or reclining.[96]

This is the state we should aspire to attain. The Prophet, peace upon him, is our exemplar. He brought a light into the world. We should try our utmost to keep that light shining.

The Prophet, peace upon him, said, "Those who will be sitting in the company of God on the Day of Judgment, are the subservient, humble, fearful people who remember God much."

We have briefly discussed the importance of humility. Here Imam al-Muhasibi mentions one of the benefits of humility which was also mentioned by Imam Ibn Qayyim, namely, nearness to God in the Hereafter. All of the qualities mentioned here are extremely important for anyone desiring Paradise. However, humility is of particular import in this regard. God mentions in the Qur'an, *This is the home of the Hereafter that we have made for those who do not desire to exalt themselves in the world, or to work corruption therein; and the end will be for the God-conscious.* (28:83)

Be sincere with God and His messenger, and give sincere advice to the believers. Consult those who fear God in your affair. God mentions, Rather, of His servants, the knowledgeable one's fear Him. (35:38)

We should take our religion, our knowledge, our advice, and admonition in all of our affairs from people who have manifested a fear of God. Why? God says, *Rather, of His servants, the knowledgeable ones fear Him.* (35:28) Hence, fear is an essential aspect of real knowledge, for all knowledge starts with God. When we seek advice from such people, they are going to advise us based upon firm knowledge. Their fear of God will prevent them from speculating based on their whims. Again, we should follow their way.

We should not hesitate to give sincere advice to the extent of our knowledge and capability. Our sincerity should be a function of our relationship with God and a function of our love for the believers. Just as we would love to receive truthful and sincere advice from others, we should love to give the same. This is an essential aspect of our religion. The Prophet, peace upon him, mentioned in that regard, "None of you truly believes until he loves for his brother what he loves for himself."[97]

The Prophet, peace upon him, said, "The religion is giving sincere advice." Similarly, one should be sincere to the leaders of the Muslims by giving them sincere counsel.

The foundational text in this area of our religion is the hadith of the Prophet, peace upon him, which states, "The religion is sincere advice." We said, "To whom." He said, "To God, His Scripture, His Messenger, to the leaders of the Muslims, and to their ordinary folk."[98]

What does it mean to be sincere to God? It means to undertake one's duties in the most perfect form possible—internally and externally. It means to fulfill one's obligations, to avoid the prohibitions, to give preference to God's pleasure over one's own pleasure.

To be sincere to the Book of God is to love it intensely, to be regular and consistent in its recitation, memorizing as much of it as one possibly can, to beautify one's voice when reciting it, to reflect on its meanings, to act on it, and to teach it to others.

Sincerity to God's Messenger, peace upon him, is to love him, to affirm the truth of his message, to obey what he commands and to avoid what he prohibits, to study his life, to adorn oneself with his way, to imitate his character and etiquettes, to teach his way to others, and to defend his honor, in a manner consistent with his example.

To be sincere to the leaders of the Muslims is to pray for their guidance and for their adherence to the proper path of religion and rectitude, to help them to rule and judge with justice and equity, to advise them of their responsibilities to the faithful, to work for the reformation of their shortcomings and mistakes, to rally the community around them and refrain from rebelling against them, as long as they do not manifest what constitutes open disbelief—and even then, to refrain from rebellion if it will result in a greater tribulation for the community.

To be sincere to the ordinary Muslims is to love for them what we love for ourselves, to reverence their elderly, to be merciful to their youngsters, to take delight in what pleases them, to be saddened by what saddens them, to pray for the continuation of their blessings and the lifting of their tribulations, to refrain from slandering them, to assist them against their enemies, to teach their ignorant, and to prefer their company to the company of others.[99]

Know that the one who has given you sincere advice has displayed love for you.

In Islam, we have tests that indicate the existence of abstract qualities. Actions are the measure of true faith. Sound faith will give rise to sound actions. One test of love is sincere advice. You give sincere advice to those you love. Your love for them does not allow you to stand idly by while they engage in actions that will lead to their ruin. Hence, when we ourselves receive sincere advice from others, they have displayed their love for us.

Conversely, one who has displayed a false face to you has betrayed you.

Why is this so? *Nasiha* is sincere advice. To display a false face (*dahana*) literally means to paint over something. In this context it means to hide what you really feel, to paint over your true feelings, to refuse to manifest your honest thoughts. So, if you see your brother deviating from the path of truth and guidance, and you refuse to let him know how disappointed you are with him, you have in fact betrayed him; in the sense that you have not attempted to correct behavior that will lead to his punishment in Hell. In this sense, you have become his enemy.

One who does not accept your sincere advice is not your brother. 'Umar bin al-Khattab said, "There is no good in people who do not give sincere advice, and there is no good in people that do not love those who offer sincere advice."

This is one reason many of our Muslim countries are in such a pathetic state. People can not give sincere advice. If you give sincere advice to the rulers you end up in prison, or worse. If you give sincere advice to the scholars, in many instances they will question your qualifications, avoid you and warn their students to beware of you. If you give sincere advice to the ordinary people, they will often become arrogant and refuse to listen to you deeming that they know more than you do, and it is you who should be following their advice.

Our approach and attitude should be far removed from what we have mentioned here. Instead of attempting to marginalize or dismiss those who present us with sincere advice, we should love them. They are people that love us and desire for us what they desire for themselves. They are people who want us to gain Paradise. They are working for our well-being. They truly love us.

Why is there no good in people who do not accept advice? Because this is one of the characteristics of the people that God condemned in the Qur'an, *He turned away from them and he said: 'O My people! I have tried to deliver the message of my Lord to you and I have given you sincere advice. However, you do not love those who advise with sincerity.'* (7:79) Thereafter, God destroyed them.

Prefer the truth in every situation and you will benefit.

The truth is a source of light and guidance. Our existence in this world is to a large extent, exposure to its vicissitudes as a test of our truthfulness. We should be true to God, self, and others as we move down the road of life. If we are able to do so we will always benefit from our circumstances, no matter how trying they are. God mentions in the Qur'an, *Do people think that they will be left alone to simply allege, 'We believe!' and then not be tested? We have tested those who preceded them in order that God will show which of them are truthful and which of them are liars.* (29:2-3)

Move away from excessive extremes and you will be safe.

God has established a delicate balance to govern everything in His creation. Moderation in our affairs is desirable because it helps us to maintain the balance God has established.

Excessiveness is destructive. So avoid excessive eating, your health will be safe; avoid excess talking, your heart will be safe; avoid excess sleeping, your worship will be safe. One of the great blessings of Ramadan is that it helps us to cut down on all three of these ruinations. We sleep less because of the *Tarawih* prayers and getting up earlier than usual to take the pre-dawn meal. We eat less because we are fasting, and if we are cognizant of the etiquettes of the fast we talk less. This is a wonderful practical exercise for us, and it endures for one twelfth of the year.

"Verily, honesty leads to righteousness and righteousness leads to the pleasure of God, Most High. Lying leads to licentiousness and licentiousness brings about the anger of God."[100]

As we mentioned, we must be true to God, ourselves, and others. Honesty leads to the pleasure of God. Honesty is one of the defining characteristics of a believer. The Prophet mentioned that a Muslim can be many things, but he cannot be a liar.[101] Hence, honesty is one of the indispensable provisions we must take along for our journey to God. One of God's names is the Truth (*al-Haqq*). It is not coincidental that honesty is one of the greatest provisions we take along for our journey to God, the Truth.

Lying destroys the ethical ideal that our religion is predicated upon. Once an ideal is gone, all of the actions that are associated with the attainment and maintenance of that ideal become meaningless. This is why a Muslim cannot be a liar, for one who lies constantly has no higher ethical standard and only looks for the means to advance his or her interests. If lying serves to advance those interests he or she readily resorts to lying. Such an approach to life is the essence of hypocrisy, for a hypocrite is a person who lives a lie. Thus we find that no one is more subject to the anger of God than the hypocrites. God mentions in the Qur'an, *Surely the hypocrites will be in the lowest level of the Hell.* (4:145)

'Abdullah ibn 'Abbas said, "Do not talk about things that do not concern you, and leave much of what does concern you. And do not argue with fools or clement people. Only mention your brother in ways that you would love to be mentioned."

What concerns us is what has some benefit sanctioned by the divine law. What concerns us is what assists us towards the attainment of Paradise. If our speech does not contain anything beneficial, we should remain silent. The general ruling for our tongue is silence. We should only move away from any general ruling for a valid reason. Hence, we only move away from the state of silence for a valid reason. Those reasons include, in some instances, various forms of joviality.

The Prophet, peace upon him, told jokes, but he never lied to do so. He worked to lighten the mood in many cases; he played with his wives. He had races with them and amused them. He also experienced lighter moments with his Companions. He is the best of guides. Hence, there is nothing wrong with having a sense of humor, as long as one's humor is not constant and it does not become frivolous.

When you argue with a fool you are wasting your time. He does not have the mental capacity to understand your arguments. In the exchange he may recast your arguments in such a convoluted form that you yourself become confused and lose the ability to even make a coherent point.

When you argue with clement people, even if they disagree, if they feel there is no legally countenanced interest to be served in refuting or correcting you, then out of respect for you or out of shyness they may simply choose to listen to you. However, they are not going to accept a baseless or weak argument. In any case, you are wasting valuable time which could have been used to do something beneficial for your soul. Life is far too short to be wasting valuable time. We have to get on with our life's work and keep moving on the road leading us to God.

Do not talk about people in negative ways. To do so is only to invite the same upon ourselves from the tongues of others. As we have mentioned, the proper course of action for us in terms of our speech is silence unless there is an interest to be served by talking. Therefore, we should "speak well or remain silent." To do otherwise is to expose ourselves to being guilty of backbiting, slander and other actions which are not only grave sins of the tongue, but also grave transgressions against the rights and honor of others.

Undertake the action of a person who knows that he will be rewarded with good, and that he will be taken to task for his transgressions.

Everything we do in this world involves recompense. Usually, that recompense is in kind. If we do good to others we usually receive good from them in exchange. If we abuse them they might be inclined to look for ways to abuse us. However, in our interactions with God, we are always recompensed in kind. He mentions in the Qur'an, *Is the reward for good ever anything other than good?* (55:60)

If we do good in our relationship with God, self and others we will always be rewarded with good. Similarly, if we behave recklessly and abusively in our relationships we are subject to be punished by God. We should live our lives in recognition of this fact.

Nothing we do is hidden from God. He knows what we do openly and secretly, by night and by day. People who are spiritually alert realize this. God mentions in the Qur'an, *It is the same were you to hide your speech or openly declare it; whether you are concealed in the depths of the night, or walking about during the day.* (13:10)

The Prophet Abraham, peace upon him, prayed to God, *Our Lord! You know what we conceal and what we reveal. Absolutely nothing in the Heavens or on Earth is hidden from God.* (13:38)

Again, these are not empty facts presented to us for mere reflection. They are pressing realities that should inform the way we live our lives. God-consciousness is only real when it informs our lives and impacts on our behavior in a positive way. In a world where people are moving further from the prophetic ideal in both subtle and open ways—in terms of character and internal states—we should work all the harder to be people who work for the revival and perpetuation of that ideal.

CHAPTER THREE

Be constant in giving thanks.

The more we give thanks, the more God will increase us in His blessings. He says, *If you give thanks, I will increase you.* (14:7) Knowing this should help us to keep our spirits high, because we know that all we must do for the perpetuity of God's blessings in our lives is to show our appreciation for them.

Imam al-Muhasibi's comment here also reminds us of the importance of consistency in our actions. We should not only be consistent in giving thanks, we should endeavor to be consistent in all of our actions. The Prophet, peace upon him, has mentioned in this regard, "I swear by God, He does not tire of your deeds, rather it is you who become tired; and the best religious acts are those that the worshiper performs consistently."[102]

Limit your expectations.

Do not expect to live a long time. On the basis of such an expectation we may engage in some extremely dangerous forms of procrastination. We might think, for example, "I'll go to Hajj when I'm fifty years old." "I will start wearing the *hijab* when I get married." "I'll grow a beard once I graduate." Do not fall into such a delusional state. Tomorrow is promised to no one. We may never see our fiftieth birthday. We may not get married. We may not live long enough to graduate.

Cut short your expectations in the world. Work as if you are going to die today. The Prophet, peace upon him, mentioned, "Exist in the world as if you are a stranger or a wayfarer and consider yourself among the inhabitants of the grave."[103]

Visit the graves with single-minded focus. They will remind you of death.

The Prophet, peace upon him, visited the graves. He would visit the martyrs of Uhud every Friday morning. Visiting the graves helps to soften our hearts. We should wash our dead relatives. We should not rely on the local "Janazah" team. The male family members should put the body in the grave. All of this reminds us of our death. In this country most of us seldom think of death as we rarely see a corpse, even though death is all around us. When the reality of death is removed from our lives it becomes very difficult for us to live for the Hereafter.

Take a journey to the place of the Resurrection in your heart.

As we mentioned in the introduction, Imam al-Muhasibi wrote a book called, *Kitab al-Tawahhum*, which is an imaginary journey to the Hereafter. Imagine that your death has occurred. Imagine the people throwing dirt on your grave. Imagine that you are lying in your grave. Imagine being resurrected and brought forth to the place of the great gathering (*al-Mahshar*). Imagine the sweat rising up to people's clavicles, up to their chins. Imagine your account being read.

Such imaginings will help to imprint the reality of death and the realities associated with the afterlife on your heart. A lot of Muslims do not think about these things and they become very distant and abstract. In such a state their impact on our behavior becomes minimal. For this reason reflection on the reality of death is one of the most important aspects of our religion. It is not coincidental that Imam al-Ghazali concludes his magnum opus, *Ihya' Ulum al-Din* (The Revival of the Religious Sciences) with a chapter entitled, "Remembering Death and What Follows It."[104]

God reminds us in the Qur'an, *Say, the death you are fleeing from will surely meet you...* (62:7) The Prophet, peace upon him, urges us, "Be frequent in mentioning the thing that will cut off all worldly delights."[105] Imam al-Ghazali mentions:

It is fitting for one who will have death as his end, dirt as his bed, worms as his companions, the grave as his repose, the bowels of the earth as his resting place, the Resurrection as his appointment, and either Paradise or Hell as his final destination, that he constantly thinks of death.[106]

Abu Dharr, mentioned, "Work as if you see [God] and consider yourself among the dead."[107]

Working as if one actually sees God is the essence of inner excellence in religion (*Ihsan*). The "seeing" mentioned here does not refer to physical sight. That is one reason the Prophet, peace upon him, said in the Hadith of Gabriel, "...as if you see Him." His wording indicates that this is not a physical vision. Rather, it involves the sight of the heart not that of the eyes.

When we consider the awe-inspiring, incomparable beauty of the Beatific Vision, which will be the greatest joy in Paradise, we understand that it will engender such love for God that were we asked by him to do anything, that task would not burden us in the slightest way. This is what Abu Dharr is saying. Undertake the actions of one whose heart is flowing over with the love of God.

We have previously commented on this expression, which is taken directly from the hadith of the Prophet, peace upon him. To add to what we have mentioned earlier, know that your death has been ordained. Imagine the whole of humanity standing shoulder to shoulder in one line and then marching forward in total darkness. In front of each and every one of us is a deep hole at varying distances and none of us know when we will drop into it. The darkness is this world and the distance between us and those holes are our life spans. We do not know when, but sooner or later we are all going to fall into the hole in front of us. That hole is our grave.[108]

Know that wickedness is not forgotten and that good does not fade.

We will be remembered by those succeeding us in this world by our words and by our actions. If our words and deeds are good then we will be remembered in a most excellent way. If our deeds are wicked then people will remember us for our wickedness. Genghis Khan certainly did some good. The Mongols, in fact, had an advanced moral code. However, his name will be forever associated with pillage, plunder and wanton death and destruction.

Most importantly, everything we do is known and will be preserved by God. He reminds us, *Whoever does the smallest amount of good will see it, and whoever does the smallest amount of evil will see it.* (99:7-8)

Nothing will escape God and He will recompense us in full for everything that we do. We should be ever mindful of that fact. He mentions in a divine hadith:

Rather it is your actions that I reckon for you and then I recompense you in full for them. Therefore, whoever finds good let him praise God, and whoever finds other than that, let him blame no one but himself.[109]

Know that a brief act that enriches you is better than a grand act that is a source of oppression.

One of the great ironies of life is that the more we waste time in counterproductive matters, the more means we will find to waste yet more time. For example, if we frequently watch television, we will always find advertisements for programs that interest us. My initial intention was to watch one hour. During that hour, I saw an advertisement for another extremely interesting program that is two hours long. So I watched the second program. Since I stayed up at night an extra two hours watching the second program, I have to take a nap after *Fajr* when I normally read the Qur'an for half an hour. Hence, it would have been far better for my soul if I had passed up the three hours of television, gone to bed on time, and then read the Qur'an for half an hour.

One of the things that we pray for is that God suffices us with that He has ordained from that which He has proscribed. If we can be content with doing those things that have a direct bearing on our attaining Paradise, we can easily monitor our time and maximize the benefit we take from it. If we fail to do so we should understand that we are placing our souls in tremendous jeopardy.

Perhaps a more relevant point here is that we should be content with humble actions that contain sincerity and thereby draw us near to God. On the other hand, we can do a grand act that involves obedience to God and is thereby laudable in and of itself. However, that act may fill us with conceit and vanity. Therefore, it becomes a means of our oppression. We should be constantly on guard against such an eventuality for it is one of the greatest guiles of our soul.

Beware of the prayer of the oppressed!

One of the critical conditions to our prayers is having complete sincerity to God. As long as a person can rely on human beings, believing that they can help him out of a particular situation, then his prayer might lack sincerity. However, the prayer of the oppressed, one who has despaired of being helped by any human being or agency is a prayer that is sincere. The Prophet, peace upon him, therefore warned, when he dispatched his emissaries to Yemen, "Beware the prayer of the oppressed person, because between that prayer and God there is no barrier."[110]

Overhaul your equipment.

Repair all of those things you need for the journey to the Hereafter. Put your tongue in order; put your prayer in order, stock up on night prayer, Qur'an recitation, and litanies. If your voluntary fast is like a rusty ship that has not been out on the water for a long while, tune up the engine, paint the hull, scrape off the barnacles and resume using that ship.

Take abundant provision.

Every journey has its unique requisites in terms of needed supplies and provisions. The journey to the Hereafter has its unique requisites. One of the most important is God-consciousness (*Taqwa*). God mentions in the Qur'an concerning this particular provision, *...and take ample provision; and the best provision is God-consciousness.* (2:197) *Taqwa*, as we have previously mentioned, is one of the foundational principles of our religion.[111]

Be the executor of your soul and do not make others your executor.

Take ultimate responsibility for yourself, and take your fate into your own hands. Our religion teaches personal responsibility. Our Prophet, peace upon him, mentioned, "You are all shepherds and each of you will all be asked concerning his flock."[112] We know that we will stand individually before God for judgment. We read in the Qur'an, *Every individual will come before Him alone on the Day of Resurrection.* (19:95)

We live in a time when many Muslims see themselves as helpless. This feeling arises in some instances from the complexity of modern society, from the constant negativity that is directed towards Islam and Muslims, or from the sensationalized news coverage of events in the parts of the Muslim world where we see our brothers and sisters being pushed from pillar to post with little we can do by way of direct intervention.

In light of these circumstances, many people feel their religion can only be salvaged, and they can only find direction in their life through a spiritual guide. While such a guide can help, in some instances, do not overly rely on him; you are ultimately responsible for your soul's salvation. When you are questioned in the grave the Shaykh will not be there. You are going to stand before God yourself. When the book of your deeds is read the Shaykh is not going to be there. When you pass over the bridge traversing Hell (*Sirat*) the Shaykh is not going to be there.

Take responsibility for your affair with lofty spiritual aspirations and enthusiasm and then you will benefit from the Shaykh. Do not expect the Shaykh to carry you to the Promised Land when you lack the motivation to walk towards it on your own two feet. Those who do not have a Shaykh and are already praying, fasting voluntarily, and doing litanies based on the prophetic tradition, they are the people who will benefit from the guidance of a Shaykh. As for weak and listless people who fail to undertake the basic obligations themselves; who find the motivational messages of the Qur'an and Sunnah inadequate, they will find it difficult to benefit from any amount of spiritual guidance. The Shaykh only enhances what is present. He cannot create something from nothing.

Approach your affair intelligently.

Do not react emotionally to challenging situations. Emotion has its place, and it can be extremely helpful in many situations. However, it should never prevent us from weighing the consequences of our actions. Know that the locus of religious responsibility lies in the intellect. Imam al-Marwardi mentions at the beginning of his seminal work, *Adab al-Dunya w' al-Din*:

> You should know that every virtue has a foundation and every etiquette flows from a spring. The foundation of all virtues and the spring of all etiquettes is the intellect, which God, Most High, has made the foundation of the religion and the pillar supporting the world. He has ordained religious responsibility upon its maturation and has made worldly affairs orderly based on its rulings. With it He has brought about conviviality between people despite

their varying aspirations and needs, and their distinct purposes and objectives.[113]

Now is the time for people of true intellect to assert themselves before people lacking intellect destroy the world through their shortsightedness and greed.

Wake up from your slumber!

Think about things based on the reality of every situation. Do not be deceived by superficial appearances. One who cannot see beyond a superficial level is spiritually asleep. One who fails to realize that the world is temporary and is merely a means to help us attain to God is asleep. Most of us are sleepwalking and need to wake up. A sleepwalker drifts along without purpose. He may even commit a serious crime in his state of total heedlessness. Only by waking up are we able to realize that we have strayed from the path and then find the ability to right ourselves.

You are responsible for your lifespan.

We have to give an account for every moment we have spent in this world. God mentions in the Qur'an, *Does the human think that he will be left to wander aimlessly?* (75:36) There are several explanations given for this passage:

1. Does he think that he will be left uncontrolled and free to do as he wishes with no consequences attached to his actions, neither in this world nor in the next in terms of his resurrection, accountability before God, and his being blessed with Heaven or dispensed to Hell?
2. Does he think that he will be left with no moral responsibilities?

3. Does he think that he will be left without a higher purpose?

4. Does he think that he will be abandoned and forsaken by his Lord?[114]

We have been commissioned with a great moral responsibility that governs all of our actions, those done secretly and openly. The moral responsibilities are so central in Islam that our scholars have devised a scale of ethical values that categorizes all of our actions in terms of their acceptability or unacceptability before God. That scale is summarized in the following way:

1. Obligatory (*Wajib*), a person is rewarded for undertaking such an act and punished for leaving it.

2. Highly encouraged (*Sunnah/Mandub/Mustahabb*), a person is rewarded for undertaking such an act, but not punished for leaving it.

3. Permissible (*Mubah*), a person is neither punished nor rewarded for undertaking or leaving such an act.

4. Disliked (*Makruh*), a person is rewarded for leaving such an act, but not punished for Undertaking it.

5. Forbidden (*Haram*), a person is punished for undertaking such an act and rewarded for leaving it.

At every moment we spend on this earth we are responsible to make the proper moral choice. Our failure to realize this is the basis of our debasement in the next life. This realization lies at the heart of our moral responsibility.

Abu Umama, said, "If the servant understood his Lord it would be better for his soul than his physical exertions."

It has been said that, "The contemplation of a moment is better than seventy years of worship."[115] Deep contemplation can lead us to an understanding of God faster than acts of worship that lack contemplation. One of the great objectives of this life is for us to know that there is no deity but God. When we know that fact and have internalized its meaning, the nature of our relationship with God is qualitatively changed. One of the sad testimonies of our time is that many people worship God yet have very little knowledge of Him. Such a state inevitably diminishes our relationship with God. Deep contemplation helps us to remedy this situation.

Know that whoever makes the Hereafter his ultimate concern, God suffices him in his worldly affair.

This is one of the reasons the Companions of the Prophet, peace upon him, gained ascendancy in the world. They desired God and the Hereafter, and God gave them both success in the world and success in the Hereafter. One of the early sages mentioned, concerning the world, "To leave it is to take it and to take it is to leave it."

If you chose to chase the world know that God will take it away from you. Some people will ask, "How is it then that so many wrongdoers are so prosperous in the world?" This inquiry can be answered in several ways. First of all, the world means nothing to God so He gives it freely to whomsoever He chooses. However, He only gives religion to those He loves. Secondly, the world is a source of their long-term detriment and is leading them to their ruin (*Istidraj*). Finally, it is not a source of true enjoyment and only deludes its possessors by blinding them to the real enjoyments of life. Based on this meaning, God taking the world from such people is removing the joy from their lives despite their abundance of material possessions.

It has been related in a hadith, "Relieve yourself from the concerns of the world as much as you possibly can. For

verily, one who makes the world his ultimate concern, God multiplies his concerns, and will set his poverty up before his very eyes. One who makes the Hereafter his greatest concern, God will focus his concerns, and make his wealth in his heart. No servant approaches God with his heart, honesty and truthfulness, except that God makes the hearts of the believers inclined toward Him with mercy and love."[116]

The meaning of this hadith closely reflects that of another, sounder narration, which have previously quoted:

> Whoever makes the world his greatest concern, God will divide him between his various concerns, and make his poverty self-evident. Furthermore, he will only get from the world what has been ordained for him. As for one who makes the Hereafter his greatest concern, God gives him focus in his affairs, places his wealth in his heart, and the world will be undeniably subservient to him.[117]

One of the fundamental bases of our success is focus; focusing on the fact that we were created to worship God, and to serve others. Everything else in the world should be subservient to these two facts. Once we accept that we were not created to make money, drive a particular car, marry a person who looks a particular way, find the ultimate mind-altering experience, wear a certain brand of sneaker, etc., then we will find focus. If we do not accept that we were created to worship we will chase money, cars, sneakers, men, women, drugs, clothes, and none of it will bring us any real happiness.

Not acknowledging this fact will also reinforce our powerlessness over our fate, because the ability to obtain all of the things the world can offer is ultimately based on what someone else can do for us. That is what it means to have your poverty made self-evident. In this state a person is needy in multiple ways. He needs others to provide him the means to material things, and no matter what he gets he will always need more. The world determines what is important to him.

Your ability to worship God and enter into a meaningful relationship with Him is based on what you can do for yourself, and when you do everything in your power, with complete sincerity and dedication to God then your wealth will truly be in your heart. Accepting this reality simplifies your life and allows you to begin planning constructively for the future. The real future is one of eternal bliss, preceded by a healthy share of bliss in this world, in spite of the trials and tribulation it holds. This is a function of "the world being subservient to you." You will not own the world or get everything it has to give, but you will have the power to determine those things in the world that are important to you. Hence, you will control the world and not the other way around.

What is mentioned at the end of this hadith is one of the great spiritual mysteries. That is God's ability to create love in the hearts of His servants for those He loves. He mentions in the Qur'an, *Surely, those who believe and do righteous deeds; the Merciful will make love for them.* (19:96) This love will be both the Love of God, and the love of other human beings. This is so owing to the fact that the believer is a source of good to all. He is therefore the recipient of good from others, especially those who are fair-minded and just. God mentions, by way of encouraging us towards lofty actions, *Is the reward for good ever anything other than good?*(55:60)

The Prophet mentioned in this regard:

When God loves a particular servant he summons Gabriel, "Verily, I love so-and-so. Therefore, you should love him." Gabriel then loves him. He subsequently summons the heavenly hosts and proclaims, "Verily God loves so-and-so. Therefore, you should love him." The heavenly hosts then love him. After that his acceptance is found on earth.[118]

We should note that love and mercy are the foundation of the brotherhood and sisterhood that Islam endeavors to establish among its adherents. It is the glue that holds the community of the believers together. The Prophet mentioned, "The likeness of the believers in their mutual love, mutual mercy, and mutual affection is like a single body. If one part complains of some injury, the entire body responds with sleeplessness and fever."[119]

Beware, my brother, of arguing over the Qur'an!

Arguing in general is extremely dangerous. It is one of the vilest expressions of the lower, unrefined soul. Imam al-Ghazali defines arguing as "objecting to the speech of someone else by revealing some defectiveness in it—either in its wording, or its meaning, or the intention of the speaker."[120] The Prophet has warned, "Do not argue with your brother. Do not ridicule him, and do not make him a promise and then break it."[121] "Whoever leaves an argument he can rightfully pursue, a house will be built for him in the middle of Paradise."[122]

Arguing over the Qur'an is especially repulsive for one engaging in such a heinous practice is belittling the revelation by making it subordinate to his base motives. He is also endeavoring to explain something God has withheld the knowledge of from humanity, for usually such arguments will involve the obscure passages of the Qur'an.

Furthermore, [beware] of disputing in religion!

After discussing arguing, Imam al-Ghazali proceeds to define disputing as, "A desire to silence or dumbfound [a disputant], and to lessen his stature by revealing a defect in his speech; thereby relegating him to the ranks of the intellectually inferior or the ignoramuses."[123] We should present the truth in the best of ways with the best proofs and then we allow it to speak for itself. This was the way of the early Muslims, and it is a sign of their sincerity. A sign of insincerity is sometimes found in the assumption that our view on an issue is the truth and that we have to bludgeon everyone else into submission to accept our view.

God clearly states in the Qur'an, *Say the truth is from your Lord. Therefore, let whosoever chooses believe and let whosoever chooses disbelieve.* (18:29) We are not obliged to force people to believe. We only try to present strong proofs for their consideration. It is up to them to accept the proofs we offer or to reject them.

[Beware] also of mentioning God in physical terms.

This is advice that we find repeated by the early generations of Muslims. God mentions in the Qur'an, *There is nothing like unto Him.* (42:11) This verse is the basis of the position of the early generations of Muslims who held God to be totally dissimilar from His creation and exalted above any hint of physicality. Imam Tahawi mentions in his *Creed,* "He is transcendent beyond limits, ends, supports, components, or instruments."[124] Imam Muwaffaq Ibn Qudama relates the following passage from Imam Ahmad regarding the interpretation of obscure textual passages that mention various attributes of God:

We believe in them and uphold their truthfulness
without knowing their exact modality, without knowing their meaning [as it relates to God]. We do not
reject any of them. We know that what the Messenger
of God brought is true, and we do not reject what
the Messenger of God, peace upon him, accepted. We
do not describe God with anything other than what
He has described himself with, without any physical
boundaries or limits.[125]

Imam Ahmad al-Rifaʾi, has mentioned something extremely insightful in this area. He said, "Verily, every text
in the Qurʾan and Sunnah whose literal meaning implies
physicality, is countered by a related text that negates that
implication."[126] These statements and similar ones from our
scholars indicate the degree Muslims have gone to, historically, to avoid mentioning God in terms that evoke physical images and likenesses. As Muslims we should not only
avoid discussing God in such terms, we should also endeavor to avoid disputing about the issue as such disputes
usually bring neither clear knowledge about the subject, nor
goodwill.

**Be among those God has described in the following
terms, When the ignorant address them they say, "Peace."
(25:63)**

Imam al-Muhasibi has already warned against engaging
in debates with ignorant people. Discussions with such folks
will devolve into arguments and disputes, because they will
not proceed on a basis that allows for an intelligent exchange
of ideas. The response of the spiritually refined to ignorant
and imprudent folks is rooted in the strength of their inner
state, in that God describes them, in the same verse Imam

al-Muhasibi has quoted, as those *who walk humbly across the earth.* (25:63) Their response also arises from the fact that they are aware of their priorities during the brief time they spend on the earth. Their priority lies in the worship God and trying to do good for the benefit of their souls and the benefit of others.

Adhere to proper etiquette.

Everything has its etiquette. There are etiquettes that govern our relationship with God, the Prophet, peace upon him, ourselves, and others. There are etiquettes for learning, studying and teaching. We should try to learn them all and adhere to them. The desire to observe proper etiquette in our affair is rooted in five things:

1. Upholding the sanctity of God, and the reverence of those who direct humanity to God; the Messengers, Prophets, saints, scholars, and others.
2. Having high aspirations in both worldly and religious matters.
3. Providing good, sincere service in every appropriate realm.
4. Exerting oneself to the fullest in religious matters.
5. Giving thanks for the blessings.[127]

Maintaining good etiquette is the essence of human refinement for it is only possible when one is aware of the higher aspects of human life such as an awareness of the supererogatory duties we owe to God, ourselves and others. Acknowledgment of those duties, which transcend obligatory religiously or humanly mandated duties, is the beginning of the process whereby we beautify our relationship with God, and we beautify all of those we interact with.

Distance yourself from the whims of your soul and from your anger.

One of the most destructive things for a person, and the most ruinous for his or her spiritual progress, is following the whims of the soul. For this reason one who masters such whims is promised Paradise. God mentions, *As for the one who fears the station of his Lord and guards his soul against its whims, Paradise will be his repose.*(79:40-41)

The whims of the soul are rooted in our physical, hence, our carnal nature. They pull us away from our spiritual nature. By conquering them, we assist our soul in its effort to move towards its angelic nature. The angelic nature is one that inclines towards obedience of God, as the angels are incapable of rebellion.

We are similarly warned against anger, which is one of the most destructive forces in human relations. The Prophet, peace upon him, once repeatedly counseled one of his Companions, "Do not become angry!"[128] One of the greatest dangers arising from anger is the fact that it removes our intellect. Once our intellect is removed from any situation we are trying to deal with, not only do we behave irrationally, but we also open the door for Satan to begin playing with us in ugly ways.

For this reason, when we feel ourselves being overcome by anger we should seek refuge with God against Satan. The Prophet informed us, "Anger is from Satan, and Satan is created from fire. Fire is extinguished by water. Therefore, if one of you becomes angry, let him perform ablution."[129] The Prophet, peace upon him, also mentioned, "Verily anger is an ember burning in the heart of the Son of Adam. Do you not see the redness of his eyes and the puffing of the veins in his neck? Anyone sensing anything of that let him lie down on the ground."[130]

We should also try to refrain from speaking when angry. This will prevent us from saying something we will subsequently regret. Controlling anger is one of the greatest signs of spiritual maturity.

Act on those things that cause you to be spiritually alert.

We should endeavor to remain spiritually alert in the face of the many forces in this society that seek to distract us. We mean by spiritual alertness, focusing on those things that aid us in attaining salvation. This includes our prayer and other religious obligations, as well as reflecting on the reality of death and remembering our accountability before God. It also means to be constantly engaged in the remembrance of God. Constant remembrance of God is one of those things that help to protect us against heedlessness.

Awareness of God's surveillance should be your greatest goal.

We should also try to remain ever aware of God's surveillance. This is a great door to spiritual progress. For this reason, the Prophet, peace upon him mentioned that *Ihsan*, inner excellence, involves worshipping "...God as if you see Him, and if you fail to see Him be mindful that He ever watches over you."[131] When we live in this state we are too shy before God to consciously sin. We may slip from time to time, but we will not consciously conspire to sin, if God so wills.

Take gentleness as your intimate friend.

We should try our utmost to deal with people in a gentle way. The Prophet, peace upon him, said, "Whenever gentleness is present in anything it beautifies it, and when it is absent from anything it defiles it."[132] Similarly, "God gives through gentleness what He does not give through violence."[133] As we endeavor to let people know what this religion is about, we should do so with gentleness. We should try to understand their point of view. We should seek to remove the sources of their ignorance instead of condemning them for their mis-informed attitudes and opinions. We should speak to them in the language of beauty before we introduce the language of authority. This is especially true when we are living in a time where globally Muslims have so little worldly authority, and therefore tend to respect authority and power more than mercy and gentleness.

In the Qur'an, Pharaoh is presented as the archetypical oppressor. However, when Moses is sent to him he is instruct-ed, *Speak to him a gentle word in order that he will be reminded and rendered reverent.* (20:44) This is instructive for us as we at-tempt to temper the arrogance or belligerence of some of our fellow citizens here in the West. We can not always hope to evoke positive reactions from people through the language of force and authority. Sometimes, especially when dealing with worldly powers that are far stronger than ourselves we have to speak a gentle word.

In any case, our actions should be a reflection of God's name, The Gentle (*al-Latif*). God deals gently with us. He overlooks many of our abuses and transgressions. He does not hasten to punish us. Rather, He gives us ample op-portunity to repent and to reform our errant ways. We should display the same traits in our dealings with each other.

Make deliberateness your companion.

We should never rush into things. We should approach everything we do with an appropriate level of deliberation and caution. The Prophet, peace upon him, said, "Deliberateness is from God and haste is from Satan."[134] Part of our deliberateness should involve knowing the ethical verdict for an action before we engage in it. This means knowing where that action rates in terms of its lawfulness, permissibility or prohibition.

We should also think about the long-term implications of a particular act. Sometimes something will appear to be virtuous. However, its long-term implications are condemnable. Such unintended consequences can only be known by reflection and deliberateness before acting. Considering the long-term or unintended consequences of an act is in fact a legal principle that influences the verdicts issued by a qualified jurist. This idea is rooted in both the Qur'an and the Sunnah. God says, *Do not insult those who call upon other than God as a deity, thereby inadvertently insulting God through ignorant transgression.* (6:108) The Prophet, peace upon him, mentioned to 'Aisha, "Were your people not new in Islam, I would have rebuilt the Ka'aba on the original foundation set by Abraham."[135] In both of these instances something of clear and immediate benefit is left owing to its long-term negative consequences.

Make security a sanctuary.

We should never rush to leave a situation that brings us safety and security. Only a fool who lacks understanding of the divine law underestimates the value of security. One of the gravest punishments threatened by the divine law involves the threat against those who recklessly undermine public security. God mentions in the Qur'an that security is one of the great public blessings He bestows on a people. He says, *Therefore, let them worship the Lord of this sacred house. He it is who has warded off hunger from them and has given them security from fear.* (106:3-4)

Ibn Mas'ud mentions, commenting on the verse, *Then you will be asked that day concerning the blessings*, (102:8) that "The blessings are security and good health."[136] We should realize that whenever we do not show adequate appreciation for a blessing it will be taken away. We fail to show our appreciation for the blessing of security when we work to undermine it. As Muslims here in the West, as well as in the East, we are obliged by Islam to maintain the sanctity of the public square. Once that sanctity is lost, we will suffer disproportionately and we will lose the divine protection of God.

Those who advocate acts of violence against the people of these western lands, where Muslims are a clear minority enjoying state protection, display little knowledge of Islam, politics, current affairs or history. They are also disregarding the blessing of security God has bestowed upon us, a sure step towards the eradication of that blessing. As for those who say that these western countries are a source of insecurity for many of our brothers and sisters in the Muslim world and it is fitting that we retaliate on their behalf, we counter that our rebellion will only bring greater hardships for them by substantiating the argument of those belligerent forces who claim, "If we do not fight them over there, we will have to fight them over here."

Our struggle is a struggle of ideas, a struggle seeking justice, fairness and equity. God has positioned us to fight that struggle better than anyone else. If we abandon it and adopt a struggle that is not ours, we will reap a bitter whirlwind as a result.

Make your spare time a source of enrichment.

The Prophet said, "There are two blessings that most people are cheated out of: Their health and their spare time."[137]

Make your spare time a source of benefit by using it wisely to help you in the attainment of Paradise. Once a single
breathe issues forth, it is gone, never to be reclaimed. How
many breathes have gone forth from us and we look back
with nothing to show for them. Fill every moment with an
action that will be the source of some lasting good. God reminds us, *The enduring benefit of the good deeds you do are best
as a source of reward from your Lord and are best as a source of
hope.* (18:46)

Make the world a vehicle.

We should use this world as a vehicle to convey us safely
to the Hereafter. Imam al-Shafi'i is reported to have said:

> God has perspicacious, discerning servants.
> They divorce themselves from the world,
> fearing its tribulations.
>
> They consider its state and when they realize,
> that it is not a permanent abode for any living creature.
>
> They approach it as if it were a vast sea, and they take,
> righteous deeds as their ships to traverse it.[138]

Imam al-Shafi'i, along with Imam al-Muhasibi, is reminding us that we should understand that the world is a means
to be used to journey successfully to the Hereafter. Most of
those who will fail to attain Paradise will do so because they
either forget or never understood what they should be doing
in the world. One of the most virtuous qualities of a faithful
believer is that he or she is alert, and their alertness wards off
heedlessness from them. Awareness that the world is a means

of conveyance to the Hereafter is one of the greatest qualities a believer can possess.

And make the Hereafter an enduring home.

Adam was expelled from our true homeland. However, God informed him that if he repents and does well in the land of his exile, which is this world, he can return home. The Prophet, peace upon him, similarly stated, "Be in the world as if you are a stranger or a wayfarer."[139] Neither the stranger nor the wayfarer attaches his heart to the land he temporarily finds himself in. He realizes that his home, loved ones and familiar environs are elsewhere. He longs to return to that land.

Paradise is our home, and we are just passing through this world on our way there. Like the stranger or the wayfarer, we enjoy the sights, sounds, smells and other delights we may experience along the way and we take the provisions necessary to continue the journey. However, our hearts should not become overly attached to these things so that we do not become deluded and forget about the incomparable beauty and delights to be found in our true home. This detachment is the essence of Islamic abstinence (*Zuhd*).

Hasan al-Basri said, "God has not made for the believer a source of rest or comfort other than Paradise."

This world is a place of work, toil and struggle. It is not a place of comfort and ease. God mentions in the Qur'an, *O you human! You are toiling mightily to reach your Lord and surely you will reach Him.* (84:6) He has not promised us perpetual bliss in this world, yet we are surprised or disappointed when we encounter trials and tribulations. Our disappointment is not justified for life will inevitably confront us with a wide array of challenges and setbacks. Whatever we do, we should not allow our frustration and disappointment in this world to distance us from God, and thereby miss the opportunity to obtain ultimate ease and the epitome of comfort to be found in the home of the Hereafter.

Upon attaining Paradise, all of the pain, suffering, frustration and disappointment one experienced in this world will be forgotten. The reason for that lies in the immeasurable comfort, joy and bliss found there. The Prophet, peace upon him, once mentioned a man who was more wretched than anyone who had ever lived. He knew of absolutely no pleasure in the world. On the Day of Resurrection he will be dipped into Paradise for just an instant and then asked, "Have you ever experienced any difficulty in the world?" He will respond, "No! I swear by God, my Lord, I have not."[140]

Be aware of places that lead to heedlessness.

Once we know that a particular place encourages us to be heedless, we should assiduously avoid that place. As a "ghetto philosopher" once said, "If you spend most of your time in bathrooms sooner or later you are going to get filth on your clothes." The opposing implication of this advice is to spend as much time as possible in those places which encourage you to remember God, especially the mosques. If one spends most of one's time in a perfumer's shop, the sweet fragrances will permeate one's clothing.

One of the groups of people that God will shade in the shade of His throne on a day there will be no shade except that shade is a man whose heart is attached to the mosque.[141] The more we go to the mosque seeking solace, to pray, reflect, and remember God, the more the mosque will go with us upon leaving it, for our hearts will tend to remain in the state they were in while inside of the mosque even after our bodies have physically departed from that sanctuary.

This is one of the fruits bestowed upon those who successfully travel the spiritual path. The positive states that they enter into through God's remembrance (*dhikr*) or spiritual retreat (*Khalwa*) remain with them even when they are in the midst of people who may be heedless of God.

Avoid the ambushes of the enemy.

That is to say, "Beware of the ambushes of Satan." We have to be constantly aware of the fact that this world is a battleground between us and Satan. There are booby traps and ambushes surrounding us on all sides. We have to watch where we walk and be on constant alert. God warns us, *Verily, Satan is an enemy unto you, treat him as an enemy.* (35:6)

Many people live lives that take no account of the existence of Satan and his sworn enmity to the human race. Satan has sworn that he will waylay the human being. He says that he will come at us from all directions. God mentions him saying in the Qur'an, *I will wait in ambush for them on your Straight Path. Then I will assault them from the front, from behind, from their right and their left. You will not find most of them grateful.* (7:16-17)

Ibn 'Abbas mentions concerning the various directions from which the assault of Satan will come:

> *Then I will assault them from in front,* "I will cause them to doubt the veracity of the Hereafter." ...*from behind,* "I will make them excessively covetous in their worldly pursuits." ...*from their right,* "I will confuse them in their religious life." ...*and their left.* "I will make sin alluring to them."[142]

This passage lets us know that the assault of Satan is a very serious matter. We must be on guard against it or we are sure to be assailed by him or his dupes.

Beware of the attacks of your whims (Hawa)!

Imam al-Jurjani, in his compilation, *al-Ta'rifat*, defines *Hawa* as, "The whimsical desires of the soul for the delights emanating from the carnal lusts in opposition to what the divine law has sanctioned."[143] The Prophet, peace upon him, has warned, "Your most dangerous enemy is the unrefined soul between your two sides."[144] In its unrefined state the soul is a slave of its whims. Therefore, the human who is himself a slave of his soul will be moved from one vile deed to another, for the whims of the soul arise from its carnal lusts and appetites. In this unrefined state it seeks instant gratification. It is obsessed with creature comforts. In its pursuit of these comforts, it does not stop to consider if either its actions or aspirations are consistent with the divine law.

CHAPTER FOUR

Beware of the flame of your carnal lust!

Here, Imam al-Muhasibi continues the previous point. He warns against surrendering to the temptation of the unrefined soul, which exists in complete harmony with the carnal appetites. In this state, the soul inevitably commands that which is vile. God mentions in the Qur'an, *Surely, the unrefined soul commands that which is vile.* (12:53)

Imam al-Muhasibi also reminds us with this choice of words, "...the flame of your carnal lust!" that the carnal lust is intimately associated with our passions, which are rooted in the "fire" of our souls. Hence, the color that symbolizes our passions is red. Furthermore, he warns us that following our carnal lusts without restraining them by keeping them within the limits established by the divine law, will lead to us being consumed by the fire of Hell.

Beware of the whimsical desires of your soul!

We should especially beware of pursuing the whimsical desires of our souls, even lawful ones, if they preoccupy us from something that may be more beneficial for ourselves and others. Our greatest desire should be to see God in Paradise. All of our other desires should be prioritized according to the degree to which they aid in the attainment of our greatest desire.

God mentions in the Qur'an, in a verse we have quoted earlier, *As for the one who fears the station of his Lord and guards his soul against its whims, Paradise will be his final repose.* (79:40-41)[145]

The station of his Lord referred to in this verse is the station God will occupy when the servant stands before Him for judgment. When we are in that situation before the awesome majesty of the Lord, Most High, one of the things that will comfort our souls will be the good that has accrued to us because of the effort we made to deny the soul its capricious, whimsical desires while we were in the world. This is one of the things that will assist us along the path to Paradise.

Verily, the Prophet, peace upon him, has said, "Your most dangerous enemy is the soul between your two sides."[146]

There is no enemy more dangerous than yourself because no one knows you like you know yourself. Hence, no one is more aware of your strengths and weaknesses than you. We should be aware of the guiles of the soul and work to cultivate and refine it so that it and its whims become consistent with the divine law, eliminating the bases for any form of rebellion against God. This process of spiritual refinement is one of the things that completes and perfects our faith. The Prophet counseled, "No one of you truly believes until his whims are in accord with what I have brought."[147]

When the whims of the soul are in accord with the divine law they assist the servant in his or her adherence to the law. When they are unrestrained by the divine law they become a source of self worship and self obedience. God mentions in that regard, *Have you not seen one who has taken his whims as his God?* (25:43 and 45:23) A human being is dignified and he should be spiritually strong. Following the empty whims of the soul is unfitting his dignity and his nature.

It became your most dangerous enemy due to your obeying it.

The whims of your soul only lead to your ruin when you follow them. The unrefined soul may incline towards a particular act such as illicit sexual relations, but the decision to fornicate is a conscious one that will only be realized when the person follows the whim or desire that suggests it. One of the great dangers in this society is that we are constantly being encouraged by messages such as, "Surrender to your desire." Like any enemy, the more we surrender, the stronger those desires become, and the greater the extent of their control over us.

If you desire to scream in a public bus or train, just do it. If you desire to hang your feet out of the window of a moving car, just do it. If you desire to try to seduce your neighbor's wife in his absence, just do it. If you want to use language that has historically been associated with vile and degenerate people, just do it. In such an environment, it is very difficult for a human being to mature spiritually.

Real spiritual growth and maturation only occurs when we suppress our desires and whims. By so doing, we unleash our real human potential. If the world is telling us to "surrender to your desire," which is the slogan of a place referred to as "Sin City," then we have to remind each other to control and suppress our desires.

In every matter whose truthfulness is not totally clear to you, assess it with the Book of God, the Sunnah, and the written legacy of the righteous forebears. If its veracity is still unclear to you after that then accept the opinion of one whose religiosity and intellect satisfies you.

This is our standard for accessing every affair in our religion, without exception. Our pursuit of spiritual maturation and elevation should be no different. In fact, our adherence to the methodology outlined by Imam al-Muhasibi in this passage is even more binding in the area of Sufism, for this is a religious science that has historically been more prone to dangerous positions and innovations than any other. Imam Junayd said concerning the teachings related to this science:

> Concerning anyone who does not study hadith, nor joins the gatherings of the jurists, nor takes his etiquettes from those of proven character; anyone following him will be ruined. *Say! This is my way; I call to God on the basis of knowledge, both myself and those following me.* (12:108)[148]

We should take our religion from those who meet the above criteria. The soundness of their religion is testified to by the loftiness of their character. We have been warned in this regard, "This knowledge is the very essence of religion. Consider well who you take your religion from."[149]

Know that truth has a witness in the readiness of your soul to accept it. Consider the saying of the Prophet, "Take a ruling from your heart, even if you get verdicts from qualified jurists."[150]

In many matters the ultimate jurist is the heart. This is why it is so very important to try to constantly purify our hearts, for the greater the degree of the heart's purity the more a person is inclined naturally towards the truth. Such an inclination lessens the chances of the heart's verdict being wrong.

This ruling is relevant in matters in which the jurist issues a verdict based on his personal inclinations or preferences without substantiating his opinion with any sort of proof from the recognized sources of the religion. In these cases, if the one asking for the verdict is uneasy with the jurist's opinion, he should follow his heart. However, if the jurist does substantiate his opinion with a valid legislative proof, and sound legal reasoning then most scholars are of the opinion that it is incumbent on the questioner to accept that opinion. God knows best.

Make your bodily actions subservient to knowledge.

Do not do anything until you know its ruling. Do not rush into business until you know if it is lawful or unlawful. Do not agree to anything until you know the ruling of the divine law concerning it. If we act without sure knowledge, we are not only abandoning one of the conditions of an action's acceptability, that it be done in accordance to the divine law, we will also likely cause far more harm than good to others if that action involves the rights of others. 'Umar bin 'Abdul 'Aziz mentioned, "Whoever acts without proper knowledge, what he corrupts is greater than what he rectifies."[51]

Focus your concerns by knowing just how close God is to you.

Many times we are heedless of God, and hence heedless of the divine law, because we forget just how close God is to us. In the Qur'an He mentions, *We are closer to him than the jugular vein.* (50:16) This closeness is through his hearing, seeing, knowledge and related attributes. Hence, He is aware of not only our open and secret actions, He is aware of our very thoughts.

When we combine awareness of His closeness with the knowledge that we will be held accountable for everything we do in this world, then we check our actions. Eventually, if we are blessed to progress on the path of spiritual refinement, we check our very thoughts. When this occurs we will be ever mindful of God, and this will be the source of our ability to focus on God while we negotiate our way through this world.

Stand before Him like a hired servant. You will find Him Most Compassionate, Most Merciful.

While on our jobs we try our best to do what our employer asks of us. Why? Because we want to be paid! We understand that if we fail to perform our specified job, we not only jeopardize our pay; we might even lose our job. We should be just as diligent in the work we are doing for God. He is the "biggest boss." Yet, how well are we performing the job He has commissioned us to do?

God wants us to worship Him based on the guidance He has sent through His Prophet, peace upon him. If we do that we receive compensation greater than anything anyone in this world can offer—Paradise! God mentions in the Qur'an that he has purchased our lives and wealth and in exchange we are given Paradise. (9:111) If we know that our job in this world is to worship God, and if we know that God has promised us the recompense of Paradise, then we should use our time, talent, skills, and abilities in performing that job.

The Messenger of God, peace upon him, mentioned, "The status of a servant with God is commensurate to the status of God with the servant."[152] That is commensurate to the fear, knowledge and gnosis he possesses of Him.

Gnosis is knowledge that is born from experience. We can conceptualize God as the One who restores life (*al-Ba'ith*). This is knowledge. If we are in a car accident and fall into a coma and after some days God brings us out of that coma, we now know from experience what God's ability to restore life means. This is gnosis. What was formerly an idea or a concept has been translated into experience. Now *al-Ba'ith* has a totally different meaning.

This is why one walking the spiritual path strives for gnosis. Once it is obtained our relationship with God is qualitatively different. One who truly knows God is shy before Him. One who truly knows God loves Him. One who truly knows God devotes himself or herself to him. One who truly knows God sacrifices for Him. One who truly knows God lives for Him.

Know that whoever gives preference to God, God prefers him.

When we prefer pleasing God to pleasing ourselves or others, we have made a statement concerning the purity of our faith. God mentions in the Qur'an, *Those who believe are more intense in their love for God.* (2:165) If our love for God is true then we will prefer Him to all others. This is a sign of true faith.

One of our religious principles is that what we get from God is a reflection of what we offer him.[153] He mentions in the Qur'an, *O Believers! If you help God,*[154] *He will help you.* (47:7) Hence, as Imam al-Muhasibi states here, if we give preference to God, he will give preference to us. His preferring us lies in His blessing us with his guidance, and protection in this world, and with nearness to Him in the next.

There is something we should understand in all of these ideas involving some sense of "reciprocity" with God. As the great sage Ibn 'Ata Allah reminds us, what we offer God is based on our weakness and the paucity of our resources. Whereas, what God offers us is based on His unlimited, unqualified Strength, Grace and Bounty. We should understand that there is no basis for a comparison between the two.[155]

Whoever obeys Him, God loves him, and whoever leaves something for His sake, He will never torment him with it. This is as the Prophet said, "Leave that which causes you doubt for that which does not cause you doubt."[156] Verily, you will never miss anything that you give up for the sake of God.

This passage provides us with an opportunity to mention aspects of the importance of love in Islamic teachings, specifically as they relate to God Himself. Many times we hear people who may lack a sound understanding of Islam saying that the God of the Muslims is a stern, unloving God. Some, who are either especially ignorant, or particularly devious, will even say that love is not mentioned in the Qur'an.

Here we will mention some of the manifestations of God's love as they occur in the Qur'an. First of all, one of God's names is the Loving (al-Wadud). We read, *Surely, my Lord is the Merciful, the Loving.* (11:90) Similarly, *He is the Forgiving, the Loving.* (85:14) We read further, *Verily, God loves those who do good.* (2:195) *Surely, God loves those who turn to Him in repentance.* (2:222) *God loves those who purify themselves.* (2:222) *God loves the God-conscious.* (3:76) *God loves those who manifest inner excellence in their faith.* (3:134) *God loves those who are patient.* (3:146) *Verily,*

God loves those who rely on him. (3:159) *God loves those who are just.* (5:42) *If any of you turns back on his faith, God will bring people whom He will love, and they will love Him...* (5:54)

All of these are manifestations of obedience to God, and God loves those who obey Him. Once we have left something for the sake of God that thing will never return to torment us. God will ensure that. By leaving anything for the sake of God we are essentially saying that we prefer the love and pleasure of God over our love for what we are surrendering, along with any pleasure we may find in what has been forfeited. This expression of love on our part invites the love of God into our lives. Those beloved with God find His protection. One of the things He protects us from is being harmed by something we have given up for His sake.

Likewise, when we give up something, motivated by the love of God, His love deepens in our hearts. The greater the love of God is in our hearts, the less our hearts are attached to the things of this world. Hence, when we give up something of the world for the sake of God, the void left in our hearts is filled by His love. When the love of God fills the heart there is no room for anything else. The reason for this lies in the fact that the space occupied in our hearts by the love of something in God's creation is proportionate to the size of that thing, whereas the space occupied in our hearts by God's love is proportionate the vastness of God's infinite bounty, grace and light. Is there any basis for a comparison here?

Protect your heart from having a bad opinion of people by the best possible interpretation.

Having a good opinion of others is part of our religion. We should always look for an interpretation of the actions of others that implies soundness in their religion and a good standing with God. To do otherwise is to open ourselves up to opinions that will imply sinfulness or even disbelief. Here Imam al-Muhasibi is warning us against such tendencies by reminding us to be as generous and liberal as possible in interpreting the questionable acts we see in our brothers or sisters.

By covering up the faults of other Muslims, we are inviting God to cover up our faults. The Prophet, peace upon him, mentioned in this regard: "A servant does not cover up the faults of another in this world except that God covers up his faults on the Day of Resurrection."[157] Conversely, those who assume the worse of their fellow believers and seek to discover and broadcast their faults are warned by God, *Those who love to broadcast the faults of the believers will have a painful punishment in this world and the next.* (24:19)

Repulse jealousy by cutting short your worldly expectations.

We have previously discussed cutting short expectations in the world. Here, Imam al-Muhasibi mentions one of the great benefits of so doing. Namely, it is a means for repulsing jealousy. When one does not anticipate living beyond the present moment it is impossible to think of some future enjoyment derived from a blessing taken away from a person we may envy and then given to us. Similarly, one can care little about the blessings someone else might subsequently enjoy if one is not looking beyond the moment. Both situations negate the primary motivations for jealousy.

Another great means to ward off jealousy from oneself is by wishing for God to increase the person you are jealous of in whatever quality or possession you envy them for. If you are jealous of someone's car for example, wish that God blesses them with a nicer car. Life is too short to squander our precious moments with actions such as jealousy and similar low pursuits.

Negate arrogance with the {reminders} of God's power.

It is said that whenever you feel arrogant go and stand next to a mountain. If that humbles you, think of the awesomeness of the power of the one who created the mountain and everything else in this vast creation. Then reflect on the fact that the one who has created all that we see or could conceive of has placed it under His dominion. How vast is His power and authority? In that vast dominion, who are we in reality? How much space do we occupy? How much time does our life in this world involve compared to the time that preceded us and the time that remains of the eternity that comes after our physical demise?

If we look at things in perspective we are quite small. Yet we are arrogant and refuse to realize our limitations. There is no real greatness for us without God. We come into this world completely helpless and ignorant. It is the mercy that God has placed in the hearts of others that leads them to clothe us, shelter us, feed us, and teach us. Yet we grow up and show little or no appreciation for God's mercy. Even worse, we reject God Himself! God summarizes this wretched state with the following words from in the Qur'an, *Does the human not know that we created him from a drop? Surprisingly, you see him set himself up as an open disputant with us. He presents us parables and forgets his origin.* (36:77-78) He forgets that his entrance into the world is through the same lowly channel by which urine passes out of our bodies.

Leave every action that will demand an apology from you.

We should take time to deliberate before we speak or act. When we deliberate we are less likely to do something we will have to apologize for. Hence, our actions will be more pleasing to God and less offensive to people.

We should also seek to avoid engaging in anything that will force us to have to repent to God. We should reflect on the lawfulness or unlawfulness of any action we are contemplating and then respond accordingly. If we are unsure of the ruling associated with a particular action, we should refrain from undertaking it until we have learned its ruling.

Our desire not to offend people is a function of our desire to secure good for them. This desire manifests itself in even the smallest act of kindness we can extend to others. The Prophet mentioned, "Do not belittle the smallest good you can do even if it is meeting your brother with a pleasant face."[158]

Avoid every situation that will encourage pretentious behavior.

A Muslim is not pretentious. We are who we are, and accepting that without any pretenses is something pleasing to God. One of the definitions of eloquence is bringing one's speech into conformity with the requisites of a particular situation. We do not need to embellish our speech, dress or actions in ways that present a false image of who we are for worldly considerations.

A lack of pretentiousness frees our hearts for the worship of God. We do not care what people think of us, as long as we are not misrepresenting God's religion. We are too concerned with what God thinks of us to be diverted by the opinions of humans. Imam Ahmad al-Rifa'i mentioned in a couplet:

> I do not care about one finding fault in me,
> as long as I am not blameworthy with God.
>
> If God knows the purity of my innermost heart,
> then I am not harmed by some unfounded slander.[159]

Protect your religion by following.

The safest approach to religion is through the impeccable following of those who preceded us. Our religion is characterized by a deeply conservative spirit. At its heart is following the established and approved practices of those who preceded us in religion (*al-Ittiba'*), and avoiding unfounded innovations (*al-Ibtida'*).

The ability to follow is aided by the existence of verified chains of transmission (*Asanid*). By taking the essential knowledge of the religion from those who preceded us, through verifiable chains of transmission, we guard against anyone passing some strange or unfounded idea or practice off as being an acceptable part of our religion. 'Abdullah bin Mubarak, one of the most learned of the early generations of Muslims mentioned in this regard, "Verifiable chains of transmission are a part of the religion. Were it not for [such] chains anyone could have said anything."[160]

Fulfill the trust you have been given by seeking knowledge.

Trustworthiness is one of the distinguishing characteristics of true faith. One of the implications of its meaning, in religious terms, includes safeguarding those things that have been entrusted to us. There are many realms where this is relevant in the life of a Muslim. It includes the trust of the religion itself, which we are enjoined to protect and to pass on as we received it. It also includes the honor of people, the greatest of which involves protecting their secrets. We are enjoined to protect the property people may have deposited with us. Our very bodies, senses, and our souls are all trusts from God, which we are enjoined to protect.

Imam Ibn Taymiyya explains that safeguarding the rights and responsibilities of ordinary folk in a society is part of the trust God has placed with leaders. This meaning is derived from the Qur'anic verse, *God has enjoined upon you that you deliver the trusts to their rightful possessors, and if you judge between a people that you do so with justice.* (4:58)[161]

None of those trusts can be preserved without knowledge. Therefore, Imam al-Muhasibi is reminding us of the intrinsic linkage between these two concepts—seeking knowledge and keeping trusts. When they are separated, a critical aspect of Islamic teachings is lost.

Guard your intellect by adopting the way of clement people.

What is the relationship between the intellect and clemency? Clement people do not become angry. Nothing removes the intellect faster than anger. The Prophet, peace upon him, repeatedly counseled, "Do not become angry!"[162] Anger arises from the stimulation of our passions. Passions are associated with fire. The nature of fire is its instability. Anger therefore renders us mentally unstable. This is the nature of Satan for he is created from fire. He allowed his passions, especially his anger and jealousy, to overwhelm his intellect. When we allow our passions to rule us, we are susceptible to the same fault.

The human being is created from clay. Clay is malleable and becomes firm over time. These are two characteristics of a sound intellect, it is malleable to sound guidance, and it matures over time. Controlling anger preserves the strength and distinction of the human being, his intellect. One of the greatest keys to controlling anger is bearing the abuse of people. Such forbearance is a manifestation of good character. The cultivation of good character is one of the implications of the advice given by the Prophet, peace upon him, when he counseled, "Do not become angry."

Ibn Rajab al-Hanbali, mentions in his commentary on the hadith, "Do not become angry," that two critical things are involved in the process of controlling anger:

> The first thing intended here is an implicit command to engage in those things that cultivate good character such as generosity, sharing, forbearance, shyness, humility, bearing abuse, refraining from harming people, overlooking slights and pardoning others, suppressing anger, having a cheerful face and pleasant countenance, and similar beautiful characteristics. When the soul adopts these character traits and they become second nature it automatically wards off anger when it arises.

> The second thing is not acting in a state of anger. Rather, you should struggle against your soul to get it to leave off implementing and acting on the demands of one's anger. "Verily, when anger possesses a human being it becomes the basis for his commandments and prohibitions."[163]

Let patience accompany you in every situation.

Life presents us many challenges and unexpected surprises. One of the greatest resources we have for successfully surmounting those challenges and surprises is patience. What is patience? It is restraining oneself, in light of sound intellect and the divine law, from responding in a way that might ordinarily seem justified in a particular situation.

Ibn Qayyim al-Jawziyya mentions three basic manifestations of patience:

> Patience involved with implementing the divine orders and acts of obedience until they are conveyed;

patience involved in avoiding the prohibitions and acts that conflict with the divine law in order that one does not perpetrate them; and patience involved with bearing the hardships and disasters that unfold with the divine decree in order that one does not become angered by them.[164]

Patience is indeed a virtue as it is the key to many of the objectives set forth for us in the divine law. It is one of the keys to divine assistance. God mentions in the Qur'an, *Seek the Help of God with patience and prayer...* (2:45) It is a key to leadership. God says, *We made from them leaders who guided by our command after they had patiently persevered and were absolutely certain concerning our signs.* (33:24) He mentions that one of the qualities of those who escape the general condition of loss that afflicts people attempting to lead lives divorced from divine guidance is that they *counsel each other towards patience.* (103:3)

One of the things that provide us with a clear indication of the value of patience is that its possessors will be given their reward from God in the Hereafter with no numerical limitations. God says in that regard, *Say, "O my believing servants! Fear your Lord. Those who do good in this world will have good. Truly spacious is God's earth. Rather, the patient ones will be given their recompense with no numerical limitations."* (39:10)

Maintain a constant spiritual retreat through the remembrance of God.

There are two ways we can understand this statement. The first is that we should make sure that our moments of religious isolation are accompanied by the remembrance of God. Isolation is a great aid for enhancing the spiritual alertness of an individual. One of the seven types of people that God will shelter in the shade of His throne on the Day of Resurrection is a person who remembers God in private while his eyes are welling up with tears.[165]

There are many virtues associated with spiritual retreats. Here is a summary of ten of those virtues mentioned by Ibn 'Ajiba in his masterful book, *Iqadh al-Himam*:

1. It keeps one safe from the ruinations of the tongue.
2. It protects the eyes from the ruinations of the vision.
3. It protects the heart from dissemblance and hypocrisy and similar diseases.
4. It helps in the attainment of other-worldliness and contentment with our blessings.
5. It protects from vile, unproductive companionship.
6. It frees up time for remembering God and worship.
7. In it is found the sweetness of obedience and the delight of intimate discourses with God.
8. It gives relaxation and rest to the heart and body.
9. It protects the believer's soul and religion from exposure to the vileness and disputations that arise from involvement with people.
10. It facilitates religious reflection and contemplation, which is the greatest objective to be achieved through spiritual retreat.[166]

Another meaning of Imam al-Muhasibi's expression is to maintain a state of spiritual retreat even when you are engulfed by people or in the midst of various social endeavors. This is one of the desirable outcomes of spiritual training. The heart has become conditioned by the worship and contemplation it has engaged in during times of isolation. Hence, it is never consciously separated from the remembrance of God, although the mind may wander during moments of heedlessness. In this state, you may leave the state of God's remembrance with your tongue. However, God's remembrance never leaves your heart. Strive to attain this state for it is people who are in this state that change societies.

Accompany blessings with thankfulness.

Thankfulness is one of the greatest means for the perpetuation of blessings. The essence of thankfulness is expressing appreciation for the blessings God has bestowed upon us. Imam Raghib al-Asbahani mentioned that this is of three types: "The thankfulness of the heart, which lies in acknowledging the blessing; The thankfulness of the tongue, which lies in praising the one who has bestowed the blessing; and thankfulness of the rest of the body, which lies in repaying the blessing."[167]

This latter duty is fulfilled by worship. When asked by 'Aisha why he was praying so fervently by night—until his feet were swollen and cracking—the Prophet, peace upon him replied, "Should I not love to be a thankful servant?"[168] Thankfulness owed from our bodies is fulfilled when we pray two cycles of the post-sunrise prayer (*Duha*). Imam Ahmad relates the following Hadith in his compendium of prophetic traditions:

> Every morning you awaken, there is a charity owed by every joint in the body. Your removing the harmful thing from the path is an act of charity; your pleasantly greeting people is an act of charity; every instance of your commanding some good is an act of charity; every instance of your forbidding some evil is an act of charity; your intimate relations with your wife are an act of charity." We said, "A man is rewarded for giving charity by [lawfully] exercising his passion?" He said, "Yes. Do you not think that he would be punished for exercising it unlawfully?" We said, "Certainly." He said, "Then he will be rewarded

for charity by exercising it lawfully." He mentioned some other things and then continued, "All of that can be compensated for by praying two cycles of the post-sunrise prayer.[169]

We should understand that when we show our appreciation for God's blessings, we are working for the perpetuation of those blessings. God mentions in the Qur'an, *If you give thanks, I will increase you...* (14:7) Those who are thankful are promised an increase in blessings, and that increase culminates in Paradise. On the other hand, ingrates are threatened with divine wrath.

This theme is reinforced by other verses in the Qur'an. For example, it is mentioned, *God is not going to punish you if you are thankful and possess sincere faith.* (4:147) One of the defining purposes of our lives is the manifestation of either our thankfulness or our ingratitude. God mentions in this regard, *We have shown him the path. Will he be thankful or will he be an ingrate?* (76:3)

Seek the help of God in everything.

At the end of the day all we have is God. If we can recognize that fact then we will realize that if we have God, we have everything; and if we do not have God, we have nothing. The Prophet, peace upon him, reminds us, "Whenever you seek help, seek the help of God."[170] We claim that we seek God's help every time we recite the *Fatiha*, *You alone do we worship, and from you alone do we seek assistance.* (1:5) However, we have to work to translate that claim into reality.

One who is conscious of God realizes that at the end of the day no one can help or assist him save God. If God determines that someone will be a means to bring you some help that God has ordained for you, then that help ultimately has

come from God. This is true in all of our affairs. If you believe that anyone or anything in God's creation can ultimately
help you, independent of God, then you will be placed in the
care of that person or thing. Hasan al-Basri wrote the following words to 'Umar bin 'Abd al-'Aziz, "Do not seek the help
of anyone other than God, for if you do, God will leave you in
the care of that other."[171]

Seek the guidance of God in every situation.

The Muslim is conditioned to seek God's guidance in all
of his or her affairs. We recite the opening chapter of the
Qur'an (*al-Fatiha*) repeatedly. One of the prayers that we
make when we recite in the *Fatiha* is: *Guide us to the straight
path.* (1:6) We have also been taught, by our beloved Prophet,
peace upon him, the Prayer of Guidance (*al-Istikhara*). That
prayer is recommended whenever we need God's guidance
in a significant matter. We will mention the hadith of the
Prayer of Guidance in full for the benefit of those unfamiliar
with it.

> It is related by Jabir bin 'Abdullah that the Prophet,
> peace upon him, used to teach us the Prayer of
> Guidance in all of our affairs as he would teach us a
> chapter of the Qur'an—saying: "When a matter vexes
> one of you, let him pray two cycles of non-obligatory
> prayer and then say, 'O God! I am seeking Your guid-
> ance through Your knowledge, and seeking confor-
> mity with Your decree through your power, and I am
> asking You of Your immense grace. Surely, You are
> all powerful, while I lack power; You are all knowing
> while I lack knowledge, and You are the knower of
> the unseen. O God! If You know that this matter is
> best for me in my religion, my worldly life, and my

afterlife, then decree it for me, facilitate it for me, and then bless me in it. However, if You know that this matter is worse for me in my religion, my worldly life, and my afterlife, then ward it off from me, and ward me off from it, and make good for me whatever the case may be, and make me pleased with it.'" At this point one should mention his need.[172]

If we learn this prayer and develop the habit of saying it before we make major decisions we will find an increased portion of blessings and ease in our lives.

Stop trying to reject what God has facilitated for you.

As Muslims we are taught that proper etiquette is one of the foundations of our affair. We have touched on this point earlier in this book.[173] One of the most serious breeches of the etiquette we could display in our relationship with God is rejecting what He has facilitated for us. Two of the most dangerous implications of this breech are mentioned by Ibn 'Ata Allah Sakandari in his famous *Aphorisms*. He says:

> [Concerning] your desire to be divested from the world, despite the fact that God has facilitated worldly means for you, beware that leaving those worldly means may be the expression of a hidden lust. [Concerning] your desire for worldly means, despite the fact that God has divested you from the world, beware that leaving that state of divestment may involve a descent from lofty spiritual aspirations.[174]

We should be constantly trying to ascertain just what direction God is moving us in, and then attempt to take advantage of divine facilitation by moving in that direction. Our failure to do so will only open up before us compound levels of difficulties. This is what Imam al-Shafi'i meant when he said, "Time is like a sword. If you do not cut it, it will cut you." He was not talking about wasting time. He was talking about understanding the ruling of God and His wisdom as it relates to the time you find yourself in. If you go against that ruling you will do great harm to yourself.

Constantly undertake those acts you would wish to meet God with.

God reminds us in the Qur'an, *Die not except in a state of Islam.* (3:102) This is a strong admonition for us to guard our actions and work arduously to insure that they are as pure as we can possibly render them. "God is good and pure and He only accepts that which is good and pure."[75] Think of how disastrous it would be for us to die while drinking alcohol, fornicating, engaged in a profanity-laced tirade, or viewing pornography. Then, possibly, despite a lifetime of good deeds, that is the act we meet God with. The following saying, attributed to Junayd, should cause us to reflect on this point, "If a truthful servant were to approach God for a thousand years and then turned away from Him for a moment, what he lost would be greater than what he had gained."[76] What Junayd means is that the servant's turning away from God during an instance of rebellion would negate everything he had gained during a thousand years of obedience.

We have to be ever vigilant in guarding our religion for we never know from which direction the ambush of Satan will come. We are instructed, *O Believers! Patiently persevere, make patience a weapon against your enemies, and be on guard, in order that you will be successful.* (3:200) We not only have to guard the frontiers of the Muslim homeland against the possible attacks of a transgressing enemy, we have to also guard the frontiers of our religion against the sure attacks of Satan and his dupes. Those attacks are sure to come. We must be ever vigilant.

Avoid everything you hate in others.

It is related that the Muslim is the mirror of his brother.[177] One meaning of this is that we see things in our brothers (or sisters) that we may not see in ourselves. Whenever we see something that we dislike in others, in addition to giving that person sincere advise in the best manner, we should work especially hard to make sure that no one sees that same trait in us. By showing us that trait in someone else and by showing us just how vile and condemnable it is God has done us a great favor. When we fail to act to rid ourselves of such traits, we are rejecting one of God's favors.

To reiterate, believers are people who strive to express their gratitude to God. We do not want to be like the doctor who can recognize and treat the diseases of others, but fails to address those same maladies within himself. Abu al-Aswad al-Du'ali describes such a person:

O you so busy teaching others!
It is high time that you taught yourself.

Begin with your own self and forbid it its indiscretions.
If it ceases, then you will be a real doctor.

There are those who listen to your prescriptions
and are cured by your words and find
your teachings beneficial.

Do not proscribe a vile trait and then
manifest its likeness.

It is a great shame upon you if you behave
in such a manner.[178]

Reject the companionship of anyone who does not increase your goodness on a daily basis.

This world is a journey to God. It is a very difficult journey. God mentions in the Qur'an, O *human! You are toiling to reach your Lord and surely you will meet Him.* (84:6) One of the greatest means we have to assist us on this journey is good companionship. The true value of a companion lies in his or her ability to make us better. When we find a companion undermining our standing with God, it is time to abandon the company of that person. The Prophet, peace upon him, mentioned, warning against the effects of bad companionship, "A person is on the religion of his companion. Therefore, let every one of you consider the company he keeps."[179]

Engage in your fair share of pardoning and clemency.

The ability to pardon is one of the greatest traits a person can manifest. The Prophet, peace upon him, is instructed in the Qur'an to pardon in more than one instance. The emphasis God placed on this trait in His communication with the Prophet, peace upon him, is a means of alerting us of its importance. God mentions, *Owing to the Mercy of God upon you, you were gentle in your dealing with them. Were you crude and hard-hearted they would have fled away from you. Therefore, pardon them, seek God's forgiveness for them, and consult them in the affair...* (3:159) He also mentions, *Make clemency your rule, command what is good, and turn away from the ignoramuses.* (7:199)

The essence of this teaching is that we should not be agitated by the abuses of people. We should not waste our valuable time and energy being obsessed with finding ways to retaliate against those who have offended us in some way. The Prophet, peace upon him, counseled 'Uqba bin 'Amir, "Join relations with those who cut them with you, give to those who deny you, and ignore those who oppress you."[180] Taking such an approach to life involves the very highest positive values. However, this is the sort of ethical standard Islam is calling us to. We have to elevate ourselves and constantly aspire to higher degrees of human purity and perfection.

We should also understand this is one of the greatest means to power. When we pardon for the sake of God, we will never be debased as a consequence. Rather, the opposite is true. The Prophet, peace upon him, mentioned, "God will only increase a servant who pardons, in honor."[181] Pardoning is also one of the keys to receiving God's pardon and mercy. God mentions in the Qur'an, *Let not those amongst you who have been graced with abundance take an oath that they will not assist their kinfolk, the impoverished, and those who have migrated for the sake of God. Let them pardon and overlook their faults. Would you not love for God to forgive you?* (24:22)

This verse was revealed concerning Abu Bakr. One of those who had slandered his daughter, our spiritual mother, 'Aisha, after she had been escorted into Medina by a single man after becoming separated from the caravan, was his cousin, Mistah. Abu Bakr had been supporting him and when he learned of his slander of 'Aisha, he wanted to cease his support. However, he happily accepted the advice offered by this verse, and set a great example for us by conforming to the lofty standards put forth by Islamic ethics.

God is reminding us through this verse that He will treat us as we treat others. If we are merciful and have the ability to pardon others, this is how we will be treated by God. What greater incentive could we have to be forgiving, forbearing, merciful, and clement in our dealings?

Know that a believer's truthfulness is tested in every situation.

One of the greatest tests of this life is the test of truthfulness. A believer should be ever cognizant of this. God mentions in the Qur'an, *Do people think that they will be left alone to simply allege, 'We believe!' and then not be tested? We have tested those who preceded them in order that God will show which of them are truthful and which of them are liars.* (29:2-3) We have previously mentioned this verse. Here we wish to point out that in mentioning "truthful" God uses the verb (*sadaqu*) whereas when He mentions "liars" He uses the active participle (*Kadhibin*).

The difference between the two is that the active participle indicates an intrinsic, static characteristic whereas the verb indicates renewal and repetition. This reinforces the point Imam al-Muhasibi is making here. Namely, that a believer is constantly tested and he has to literally reaffirm his truthfulness in an unending succession of situations. We should further note that truth, being dynamic, has the power to revitalize souls, restore hope, replenish hearts, and engender spiritual growth. Those who are spiritually alert readily perceive this truth. Falsehood, being static, encourages spiritual inertia, and eventually spiritual death.

He will expose himself to tribulation.

A believer does not hesitate to expose himself to trials and tribulations for the sake of the truth, because he knows that the ease and comfort he may gain in this world is nothing compared to the joy, bliss and comfort to be found in the hereafter. Correspondingly, he knows that if he were to compromise (or possibly even abandon) his religion for some worldly comfort or benefit, he would be exposing himself to the epitome of pain, torment and discomfort in the coming life.

Hence, instead of running away from the trials that occur as a result of our faith, we should embrace them and build ourselves up spiritually to face them with dignity, patience and grace. We should also know that trials and tribulations are the nature of this world. God mentions in the Qur'an, *We will surely test you with something of fear, hunger, and loss of wealth, life and fruits. Give glad tidings to those who patiently persevere.* (2:155)

He watches over himself for the sake of God.

One of the surest means to attain what Imam al-Muhasibi is mentioning here is adhering to the program outlined by Imam Ibn Juzayy al-Kalbi in his commentary on the following Qur'anic passage, *Surely, God ever watches over you.* (4:1) He says:

> When the servant actualizes the meaning of this and similar verses he achieves the station that involves the conscious awareness of God's observing him (*Muraqaba*). It is a noble station whose foundation is knowledge and a particular state of being. It subsequently yields two additional states of being. As for knowledge, it is the awareness of the servant that God is overlooking him, gazing upon him, witnessing all of his actions, listening to his every utterance, cognizant of every thought that comes to his mind. As for the particular state of being, it is his heart being constantly aware of the aforementioned knowledge to such an extent that it overwhelms him. He is never heedless of it. The knowledge is insufficient without this particular state.

When both this knowledge and state of being are attained they lead to an enhanced ontological state for the Companions of the Right Hand. This enhanced state is shyness before God. It necessarily brings about leaving sinful rebellion and a commitment to obedience. As for the enhanced ontological state it bequeaths unto those nearest to God, it is the keen perception of God through the inner vision of their hearts. This necessitates magnifying and upholding the majesty of the Most Majestic. These two fruits were indicated by the Messenger of God, peace upon him and his family, when he said, "Excellence in religion is that you worship God as if you see Him, and if you fail to see Him, verily He sees you."

His saying, "...that you worship God as if you see Him" indicates the second fruit. This is the inner vision of the heart, which necessitates exalting the greatness of God. This is like the state of one who sees a mighty worldly king. He necessarily exalts him. As for his saying, "...and if you fail to see Him, verily He sees you" it indicates the first fruit, which means if you are not amongst those possessing heart-vision, be of the people of shyness, which is the station of the Companions of the right hand.

When he (the Prophet, peace upon him) began explaining excellence in religion by mentioning the loftiest station, he realized that many people would fall short of this station. Therefore, he mentioned another station.

You should know that awareness of God's observation will not be properly attained until it is preceded by *Musharata, Murabata,* and then followed up with *Muhasaba* and *Mu'aqaba.*[182] As for *Musharata,* it is the servant making it conditional for himself to be consistently obedient and to avoid all sins. As for *Murabata,* it is his entering into a covenant with his Lord to do that. After these two, he begins to be aware of God's observation from the beginning to the end of his affair. After this he engages in *Muhasaba* by taking himself to account concerning his fidelity in implementing the conditions and the covenant he has placed over himself.

If he finds that he has been faithful in fulfilling that which he has convened with God, He praises Him. If he finds that he has failed to fulfill the condition(s), and has breeched the covenant, he engages in *Mu'aqaba* by rebuking himself so strongly that it discourages him from ever breeching the covenant again. He then repeats this process over and over until he meets God, Most High.[183]

Be steadfast in the path of truth, the people's love will come to you.

God wants us to succeed in this world and the next. He mentions in the Qur'an, *He is not pleased that His servants disbelieve.* (39:7) He has sent His Prophets and Messengers, peace upon them, as exemplars and guides for us. He merely asks us to be steadfast and upright in the path of truth. Being steadfast on the path of truth is what we must do to fulfill the deal we have entered into with God. God mentions in the Qur'an, *Surely, God has purchased from the believers their lives and their wealth. For that they will have Paradise.* (9:111) He adds, *O believers! Shall I direct you to a commerce that will save you from a*

*painful punishment? Believe in God and His messenger and struggle
in the way of God with your wealth and your lives. That is best for
you if you but knew.* (61:10-11)

In exchange for Paradise, God is requesting that we steadfastly strive and struggle for His sake. Imam Fakhruddin Razi,
commenting on the latter verse mentions:

> The nature of struggle (*jihad*), after the two men-
> tioned in the verse—with your wealth and your lives,
> are three: A struggle between the person and his soul.
> This involves disciplining the soul and denying it
> its whimsical desires for worldly delights and carnal
> lusts; a struggle between him and the generality of
> humans. This involves him leaving off craving their
> possessions, and being compassionate and merciful in
> dealing with them; and a struggle between him and
> the world. This involves him taking it as a source of
> provision for his journey back to God.[184]

Success in this struggle involves a life dedicated to God,
dedication that is manifested in righteous deeds. When one
succeeds in this struggle he or she is beloved to God. When
God loves a servant He creates love for them in the hearts of
the righteous. This meaning is applicable in this case. God
mentions in the Qur'an, *Surely, those who believe and do righteous
deeds, the Merciful will make love for them.* (19:96)

**Be truthful in your quest and you will inherit heart-
vision. The fountainheads of gnosis will appear before
you. You will be given divine facilitation to distinguish
the true value of all knowledge that comes to you.**

Truthfulness is one of the forces that propel a believer
forward in his or her quest for the Divine. The Prophet, peace

upon him, mentioned, "Surely, truthfulness leads to righteousness and righteousness leads to Paradise..."[185] This journey to the Divine, which is rooted in truthfulness, is made possible by the heart-vision that is given to a righteous person. The Prophet, peace upon him, mentioned in another hadith, "Beware of the insight of a believer for he indeed sees by the light of God."[186] This light is placed in the heart of the believer and it allows him to see those things that exist in a realm of metaphysical reality that is closed to those lacking that light.

Truthfulness is also one of the great keys that unlock the treasures that God has stored up for the believer. The Prophet, peace upon him, is related to have said, "Whoever is sincere with God for forty days he will speak from the fountains of wisdom that will spring from his heart."[187] As sincerity is inconceivable without truthfulness, this is a great gift from God to those who are truthful. The fountains of wisdom that are mentioned in this hadith spring forth from a heart that is alive and therefore is able to distinguish right from wrong. Hence, one of the greatest fruits of those who submit to divine guidance and endeavor to lead lives in light of the divine truths buttressing this universe, is their ability to be guided, by being able to distinguish right from wrong on the basis of the knowledge they possess.

This ability to distinguish the merit and veracity of things is given to a person by God. However, this great gift is one that has to be earned. In the language of the Qur'an it is known as "Furqan." God mentions, *O believers! If you are aware of God He will bestow upon you a criterion for distinguishing right from wrong, remove your misdeeds, and forgive you. Surely, God possesses boundless grace.* (8:29)

CHAPTER FIVE

Advancement is for one who strives.

God mentions in the Qur'an, *Surely, a person will only have what he strives for, and all of his strivings will be shown.* (53:39-40) In this verse, God reminds us that just as no person will be responsible for the deeds of another, a person will only benefit from the deeds he has himself undertaken, generally speaking. Therefore, anyone sincerely desiring to advance on the spiritual path has to undertake the actions that lead to advancement. This striving is important at every stage of the aspirant's journey, from beginning to end. The ultimate objective of the spiritual path is the successful meeting with God. One of the most beautiful and concise phrases in that regard, one that is consistent with what Imam al-Muhasibi states here, is the following verse, *As for one who hopes to meet his Lord, let him perform righteous deeds, and join no one in worship as a partner with his Lord.* (18:110)

Diligent striving at the beginning of the path indicates that a person will make it successfully to the end of the path. Ibn 'Ata Allah mentions in his *Aphorisms*, "Whoever has an enlightened beginning, will have an enlightened end."[188] One meaning of an enlightened beginning is the light that appears on the face of a devoted servant, who exerts herself diligently in worship. One meaning of an enlightened end is the radiance appearing on the face of a servant entered into the divine Presence at the time of the Beatific Vision. God mentions in the Qur'an, *Faces will be radiant that day, gazing towards their Lord.* (75:22-23)

Reverence [of God] is for one who knows.

God mentions in the Qur'an, *Rather, of His servants, it is the knowledgeable that reverence God.* (35:28) Much has been written about this verse and the relationship between knowledge and reverence. One of the most powerful passages I have found in that regard was penned by the Qur'anic scholar, Yusuf Ali. He writes commenting on this verse:

> In outer nature we can, through colors, understand and appreciate the finest shades and graduations. But in the spiritual world that variation or graduation is even more subtle and more comprehensive. Who can truly understand it? Only God's servants, who know, i.e., who have inner knowledge which comes through their acquaintance with the spiritual world, —it is such people who truly appreciate the inner world, and it is they who know that "the fear of God is the beginning of wisdom."[189] For such fear is akin to appreciation and love,—appreciation of all the marvelous beauties of God's outer and inner world ("God is exalted in Might") and love because of His Grace and Kindness ("Oft-Forgiving).[190]

Unfortunately, in our day many people have been veiled from God. Because they have been veiled from Him they do not know Him, and because they do not know Him, they do not fear Him. Such people have been described by the great sage Ibn 'Ata Allah Sakandari in the following words, "He has been veiled from the light of spiritual knowledge by the clouds of material existence."[191] The veiling of such a person lies in the fact that everything in this physical world points to the existence of a wise creator. One who cannot see beyond the creation to witness the existence of its creator has been veiled. That veiling in and of itself constitutes a proof for God, for God's existence is so self-evident, He is the only force powerful enough to veil Himself from His creation.

Reliance is for one who trusts.

Trust (*Tawakkul*) in God is defined as relying on God to bring good and to ward off harm in both worldly and otherworldly affairs. Reliance on anyone only comes when we trust them. Hence, Imam al-Jurjani defines *Tawakkul* as, "Trusting in that possessed by God while despairing from that possessed by people."[192] At the heart of this definition is trust.

If we fear someone will let us down or disappoint us, we will not rely on them. God will never disappoint us, although we often disappoint ourselves in our dealings with Him. God never fails to deliver on what He promises. If we take a deep and sincere look at our lives we will discover this truth. As any object of our trust other than God is dependent on Him, for both its existence and its actions, ultimately we have to trust in God. In this sense, there is a deep truth embodied in the Qur'anic verse, *If anyone trusts in God, God suffices him.* (67:3)

However, we should also understand that a critical aspect of trust is taking the means needed to insure a positive outcome in a particular endeavor. Imam Tirmidhi relates an incident in which a man came to the Prophet, peace upon him, and said, "Should I tie my camel and trust in God or should I leave it unfettered and trust in Him?" He responded, "Tie it and trust in God."[93]

Fear is for one who is certain.

We normally do not fear things that we are uncertain about. This is one of the reasons a child has to learn that fire burns or bees sting. Their lack of knowledge creates situations where they are exposed to severe danger in many instances. Through our worship, we become more and more certain concerning God, because our maturing spiritual state allows us to see ever more and deeper manifestations of God's attributes and names, along with His power and His degree in all that surrounds us. All of this leads to greater certainty about His existence, His promise, and His threat. The certainty of His promise enhances our love, and the certainty of His threat enhances our fear.

Increase is for one who is thankful.

The statement here of Imam al-Muhasibi is the expression of a spiritual law, a law that is expressed in the following verse of the Qur'an, *When your Lord proclaimed, If you give thanks, I will increase you. If you are ungrateful, you should know that my punishment is severe.* (14:7)

We should thank God for every good that we enjoy. By doing so, we should be assured that God will increase that good. The most fundamental way that we thank God for his blessings is through our worship of Him. This was illustrated by the Messenger of God, peace upon Him. God blessed him in ways no human being before or after him was blessed. He expressed his thanks for those blessings through his worship, as we have previously mentioned.[194]

You should know that whatever [understanding] the servant obtains, it is proportionate to his intellectual sagacity, the existence of his knowledge, and his consciousness and obedience of God.

The three foundations for advancing in Islam both spiritually and intellectually are: a sound understanding of the religion; a sound intellect and beneficial knowledge. The Prophet, peace upon him, mentioned in that regard, "Whoever God desires good for; He gives him a sound understanding of the religion."[195] A sound intellect provides the parameters that govern our potential for acquiring knowledge—under ordinary circumstances. Knowledge, in turn, allows us to obtain an accurate idea of what we need to do to bring our lives into conformity with the divine law. Understanding allows us to act judiciously in undertaking the measures we must engage in to implement that knowledge. Knowledge allows us to know what must be placed in the scale. Understanding provides the means to insure that the scales remain balanced.

The greatest fruit of these three gifts is the awareness that there is no god but the one true God and that it is incumbent upon us to serve God by obeying His commandments and avoiding His prohibitions in a spirit of faithful and dutiful obedience. This is the essence of true religion. Those who attempt to separate consciousness of God from the incumbency of obeying Him are engaged in a futile exercise that will yield little in the way of real spiritual maturity.

Upon whosoever God bestows the gift of sound intellect, enlivens with knowledge after bestowing faith upon him, bestows heart-vision through certainty, and gives insight into his own faults; [for such a person] God has facilitated all of the characteristics of righteousness. Therefore, seek righteousness through God-consciousness, and take knowledge from reverent people.

Once a person has been given a sound intellect and uses it to arrive at a position of firm faith, he or she has entered upon the path leading to spiritual maturation. That maturity will bear the fruit of righteousness. Therefore, any person who desires to live a righteous life must first cultivate a healthy consciousness of God. To be healthy that consciousness must culminate in a willing propensity to implement the divine commandments and avoid those things God has prohibited. A person able to do that will lead a righteous life filled with good, for as God declares in the Qur'an, *He has made lawful for you the good and pure and he has forbidden for you vile things...* (7:157)

Knowledge in turn, is integral to this process, for as we have mentioned, it allows us to obtain an accurate idea of what we need to do to bring our lives into conformity with the divine law. Therefore, true knowledge is found with reverent people, for their lives have been brought into accords with the law of God.

Seek certainty by means of sound investigation in places conducive to contemplation. God mentions in the Qur'an, Thus did we show Abraham the unseen wonders of the heavens and earth in order that he would be among those possessing certainty. (6:75) The Messenger of God, peace upon him, said, "Learn certitude! Verily, I am learning it."[196]

Certitude is a sign of true faith. Its possession is one of the qualities that God places in those He chooses to lead nations on the basis of His command. He mentions in the Qur'an, *And We made from them leaders who guided by Our command after they had patiently persevered, and they were absolutely certain concerning our signs.* (32:24)

The advice here is for us to seek to purify our hearts, for it is there that God will show us aspects of His creation that our physical vision is incapable of perceiving. God will not convey us to the heavens, nor will He split the Earth in order to show us the unseen wonders lying therein. However, He will convey those wonders to our hearts, and one witnessing them will be absolutely certain concerning God thereafter.

The fact that Abraham was shown those wonders does not mean that he was not among those possessing certitude. Similarly, the fact that the Prophet, peace upon him, was "learning" certitude does not mean he did not possess it. It means that they were both being brought to ever higher decrees of certitude.

The Prophet, peace upon him, who is our teacher and exemplar, described himself as learning certitude. This is instructive to us, for as he learned it, his heart was being purified. The greater the degree of purity the more he was shown of the unseen wonders. The more he was shown of the unseen wonders, the greater his certitude. Although we will never come close to the degree of certitude he possessed, if we cleanse and purify our hearts, we will be able to see more of those wonders and to thereby grow in certitude.

Know that every intellect not characterized by three things is a source of treachery: It prefers obedience to sin; it prefers knowledge to ignorance; and it prefers religion to the world.

The intellect is a great gift to humans from God. However, like all gifts, it can be fully appreciated and used in a positive or constructive way, or it can be used for negativity, harm and vice. An example of this is Satan. He rationalized that he was better than Adam. Hence, by his calculation, it was he who was deserving of God's greatest favors and not Adam. Satan misused his intellectual powers because he was unable to escape the power of his passions and lusts. He was thus trapped, in terms of his analytical ability, at the level of physicality and was incapable of seeing divine truths whose existence is only discerned through heart-vision.

Because obedience to the Divine, beneficial knowledge and true religion all require a person to restrain himself, they call for an active struggle against, and eventually vanquishing the lower desires. This is one of the great struggles in this world and God rewards greatly the one undertaking it. God mentions, *As for those struggling for our sake, we will guide them in our paths.* (29:69)

Any knowledge not characterized by three things increases the proof against you: It prevents you from harming people by cutting off your desire for what they possess; it leads you to act with humility; and it leads you to give your utmost for the sake of fairness and mutuality.

We are instructed by our Prophet, peace upon him, "Divorce yourself from the world and the people will love you."[197] One of the benefits that accrues to people who are able to divorce themselves from the world is they earn love from people. This is for several reasons. First of all, an individual divorced from the world does not transgress against people and has no ulterior motive for harming them in any way. That being the case, her unadulterated desire is to treat people well.

Secondly, the greater an individual's divestment from the world, the greater will be her capacity to love God. This is so because a heart that is darkened over by images of the world will have little space from which to reflect the divine light. A heart that does not reflect the divine light will not be able to perceive the beauty of God. A heart divorced from the beauty of God lacks the most fundamental basis for loving God. The opposite is true for a person divorced from the world. Such a person will love God and that love will lead to an interest in those things loved or valued by God. One of the valued things is refraining from harming others and working for their benefit. These meanings and understandings are closely related to a person's knowledge of the religion.

True knowledge also leads to humility. One reason for that is the fact that true knowledge opens up ever deeper realms for understanding just how much one does not know. A person who lacks even a rudimentary knowledge of physics has no basis for knowing the intricacies of the special theory of relativity, anti-matter or string theory. It is only his knowledge in the first area, basic physics, which leads him to understand that he lacks knowledge in the latter three. Such is our knowledge of Islam. As we learn more, we are humbled for we realize just how much we do not know.

True knowledge of God also leads to confidence in His promise. One of the things He has promised, as His Prophet, peace upon him, makes clear, is that one who humbles himself for the sake of God will be elevated. His Prophet, peace upon him, mentions, in a hadith we have previously cited,[198] "No one humbles themselves for the sake of God except that God elevates them."[199]

True knowledge also leads to implementation. In this regard, we are commanded by God, *Be upright for the sake of God; witnesses for the truth, even if it be against yourself, your parents or your kith and kin.* (4:135) A knowledgeable Muslim is a person committed to justice. One of the fruits of justice is mutuality, which is also a great, if oftentimes neglected, aspect of our religion. As Muslims we are enjoined in the Qur'an to cooperate for goodness and righteousness (5:2); we are advised to build our affair on mutual consultation (42:38); we are described as encouraging each other with truth and patience (103:3); we are described as constituting a solid cemented wall in the face of those displaying enmity towards God and His Messenger. (61:4)

You should know that no one has adorned himself with anything as beautiful as the intellect. No one has worn a garment more beautiful than knowledge. [This is so] because God is only known through the intellect, and He is only obeyed with knowledge.

One who realizes the beauty of the human intellect realizes the degree to which humans have been distinguished through our intellect from the balance of creation. The cognitive superiority of a human compared to the most intelligent ape, deemed by evolutionists to be our distant cousins and closest likeness in the animal kingdom, is so great that it leaves no basis for a meaningful comparison. God has made the possession of this great gift the locus of religious responsibility. Therefore, one who loses his or her intellect, due to sleep, unconsciousness, insanity, or illness is no longer religiously responsible.

One recognizing this gift seeks to cultivate it and to utilize it in the best of all possible ways. It beautifies the person because he or she realizes that the intellect is their path to not only knowing God, but to worshipping Him. Nothing ennobles and beautifies a person more than these things: the knowledge of God, the knowledge of His beauty, and the knowledge of how to properly undertake His worship. The knowledge of God reveals His beauty. This in turn allows one possessing that knowledge to endeavor to reflect that beauty, while His worship ennobles and further adorns the human being.

The relationship between the realities mentioned in the previous paragraph can be summarized by two prophetic hadiths: The first is, "Verily, God is beautiful and He loves beauty."[200] The second is, "Verily, God is good and pure and He only accepts the good and pure."[201] Purity is one of the most common characteristics of beautiful things. Examples of this would include the unadulterated beauty of a deep blue cloudless sky; the unadulterated beauty of a crystalline stream; and the invigorating smell of the earth after a strong wind and drenching rain has cleared the air of the polluting stench of the waste generated by man and his machines.

Know that the gnostics established the principles of insight into the [soul's] states upon the witness of knowledge through God, and a sound understanding of the divine law. Will you not consider the saying of the Prophet, peace upon him, "Whoever acts on the basis of his knowledge, God will bequeath unto him knowledge that he knows not."[202] The sign of this is that additional knowledge leads to greater fear and greater adherence to the prophetic example. Whenever its possessor increases in knowledge he increases in fear, and each time he increases in action he increases in humility.

As Muslims we recognize two primary sources of knowledge, each of which is intricately connected to the other—knowledge opened up to a human being by God, and knowledge revealed by God in the divine law. The first type, which is not revelation, is the insight and understanding that God gives a servant into the unseen realities. This means subtle forms and shades of understanding that allow one to distinguish—most prominently—right from wrong.

The second type is revelation, which forms the basis of the divine law.

Proof of the first type, which some Muslims would deem controversial, is found in both the Qur'an and the Sunnah. In the Qur'an we read, *Be mindful of God and God will teach you, and God is knowledgeable of all things.* (2:282) Imam Qurtubi mentions concerning this verse:

> A promise from God, Most High, that whosoever is mindful of Him, He will teach him. That is to say, He will make in his heart a light that will allow him to understand things.[203]

This narration indicates that this type of knowledge, which the scholars refer to as divinely inspired knowledge (*'Ilm Ladunni*), only comes to those who strictly guard the commandments and prohibitions of God. Another proof of this type of knowledge is the Qur'anic verse, *O believers! Be mindful of God. He will make for you a criterion...* (8:29)

Again, it is critical to note that the knowledge that accompanies the state referred to in the previous section only comes to those who are dutifully mindful of the obligations imposed on them by the divine law. They are people who act on their knowledge. This is a crucial aspect of our religion and a prerequisite for one to be considered a true scholar, or to gain access to a deeper understanding of Islam.

Being consistent in implementing the teachings of Islam is not a light matter. We can all relate to the periods when various aspects of our devotional life left much to be desired. Ibn 'Abbas mentioned that there was no verse in the Qur'an that was weightier on the Prophet, peace upon him, than the following, *Be consistently upright as you have been commanded!* (11:112) The Prophet, peace upon him, was addressed, "It is related from you that you said, '*Hud* has made my hair gray.'"

He stated, "Yes." It was said, "What has grayed your head; the stories of the prophets, or the destruction of previous nations?" he answered, "No. Rather the phrase, *Be consistently upright as you have been commanded!*"[204]

The foundation that led to strength in their path is consistency in commanding the good and forbidding the wrong—with honesty, truthfulness, prioritizing knowledge over the desire of their souls, and finding sufficiency with God from all of His creation.

Those of us who have accepted Islam have done so for the sake of God. When we can actualize the understanding described here by Imam al-Muhasibi in our lives, we have entered upon the path that culminates in total reliance on God. The essence of this path is captured by Imam Nawawi in his litany when he states, "In the Name of God, with God, from God, to God, [relying] upon God, and through God, there is no strength or power except with God."[205] When we enter that path we can be consistent in our actions and in our obligations towards our fellow humans; for we are not so fearful that we are discouraged from acting in some situations, while in others we act readily. Such vacillation is one of the strongest factors leading to inconsistency.

One of the things our religion requires of us is to judiciously enjoin the good and forbid the wrong. In so doing, we are not to fear anyone except God. However, to fulfill this great responsibility, we have to actually know what is right and what is wrong. We also have to know when it is obligatory to enjoin or forbid good and wrong respectively, and when it is not. This requires knowledge. It also requires acting on knowledge and truth even if it means that we go against our own inclinations and propensities. Acting according to these standards is true strength and refined character.

Therefore, seek the way of people whose knowledge increased their [reverence], whose actions increased their heart-vision, and whose intellect increased their gnosis.

A person of God is thankful for the gifts he or she has received from God. As we have discussed in a prior section, God gives increase to those who are thankful. Here we mention that believers who possess knowledge, actions, and intellect—and give thanks for those qualities—are promised an increase in fear, heart-vision, and gnosis.

When we perceive those qualities in a person we should try to follow their way because the qualities we perceive in them are in reality gifts from God. Hence, they are people who are being showered with divine grace. These are truly people worthy of following; because they are receiving from God what we should aspire to be granted.

If lack of the necessary etiquette prevents you from following their way, take pause and rebuke yourself. The attributes of those who are sincere will never be lost to those possessing true knowledge.

If we find ourselves unable to follow their way, we should understand that there is something defective in our knowledge of the religion. That defectiveness in knowledge is widespread today amongst the Muslims. For example, one such proof is that scholars whose contribution to Islam, and whose truthfulness and faith have been testified to historically by the entire Muslim community are in some quarters today ridiculed, defamed, and impugned with charges of heresy.

If our knowledge is true, as Imam al-Muhasibi mentions here, we will not fail to see the positive attributes and virtue of the sincere people who preceded us. If we fail to see them, then this is evidence that God has chosen to cut us off from their good, and to deprive us the gifts he has bestowed upon them.

Know that every idea has an associated etiquette, and in every parable there is clear knowledge. Individuals able to discern this truth are those who understand what God desires, and are able to harvest the fruits of certainty from His scriptures.

The most important thing we can understand, concerning ideas, is that they should affect how we act. In Islam, which is an ethical system, there is no value to ideas that are divorced from positive action. The Prophet mentioned, "I have only been sent to perfect good character."[206] He did this with both actions and ideas. Translating ideas into good character is the essence of the ethical orientation that characterizes our religion.

Any insight that does not culminate in improved character and action, any allegory that does not culminate in clarity, as to what we are to do in the varying situations life presents to us, has no basis in Islamic teachings. One who has been blessed to understand this by seeing the relationship between the things Imam al-Muhasibi mentions here is able to be increased in certitude every time he or she reads the Qur'an because this is the essence of the Qur'anic message.

Ideas, such as love, are coupled with etiquettes, such as giving preference to others, and ensuring their needs are met before our own. *They give preference to others even though they themselves are poverty-stricken.* (59:9) Allegories, such as the allegory of the good tree, culminate in clear religious teachings, such as the importance of sound faith in our affair. *Have you not seen how God sets forth the parable of a good word, which is like a good tree whose roots are firmly planted and whose branches are in the sky? It brings forth its fruit during the proper season, by permission of its Lord.* (14:24-25)

The greatest fruit to be harvested from the scriptures is sound understanding. The Prophet, peace upon him, mentioned, "Whoever God desires good for He gives him a sound understanding of the religion..."[207] One of the greatest things we can understand about this religion, especially in these days when people of scant intellect and ill-will are attacking its law as illogical and oppressive, is that its law, as Imam al-Muhasibi has endeavored to emphasize during the last few sections, is the true basis of human excellence, virtue and purity. God mentions in the Qur'an, *God does not desire to create hardship for you. Rather, He desires to purify you and to complete his favor upon you.* (5:6)

What are the signs of this in a truthful servant? When he studies he contemplates; when he falls silent he reflects; when he speaks he mentions [God]; when something is denied him he is patient; when he is given something he is thankful; when he is tested [with a death] he says, We belong to God and unto Him we are all returning (2:156); if someone behaves ignorantly with him he bears their abuse; when he learns something he humbles himself; when he teaches something he does so with gentleness; and when questioned he responds to the full extent of his knowledge.

All of the things mentioned here illustrate good character. Their meanings are clear requiring no commentary. What we will mention at this point are some of the prophetic encouragements towards good character. He mentioned in this regard:

> Be mindful of God wherever you are, follow up any misdeed you may commit with a good deed that will eradicate it, and deal with people on the basis of good character.[208]

The most complete of the believers in faith are the best of them in character, and the best of them in character are those best in their treatment of their wives.[209]

I guarantee a house on the perimeters of Paradise for one who abandons disputing with others even when the truth is on his side. I further guarantee a house in the middle of Paradise for one who forsakes lying, even when joking. Finally, I guarantee a house in the highest part of Paradise for one possessing good character.[210]

The believer will attain via good character the rank of one who fasts perpetually and spends his nights in prayer.[211]

Righteousness is good character.[212]

The Prophet, peace upon him, was asked about what quality enters people into Paradise more than any other. He answered, "Mindfulness of God and good character."[213]

Nothing is weightier in the scale of a believer on the Day of Resurrection than good character. And God hates vile, vulgar people.[214]

He is a healing for people that seek him, an aid for those desiring guidance, a truthful ally for the veracious, and a sanctuary for the fearful. He is righteous, easy to please when his rights are involved, exceedingly impeccable when the rights of God, Most High, are involved.

This is the way we should be if we are truthful. When someone seeks our assistance we should do our utmost to help them. This is especially true if they are seeking help in their religion and we are able to assist them. We should be an ally for those seeking to fight the battle of the truthful in a world that is increasingly given to falsehood. We should try to keep ourselves around people who are both truthful and committed to the defense of the truth—by way of implementing the injunction of God, *O Believers! Be mindful of God, and keep yourselves in the company of the truthful.* (9:119)

We should not be afraid or ashamed to aspire for righteousness. We should never demand our rights in full, to be paid back a sum of money, for example, if we will not be harmed by foregoing those rights. Conversely, we should be exceedingly impeccable in conveying the rights we owe to others and especially the rights we owe to God.

His intention is better than his action, and his action has a greater impact than his speech.

Our actions are judged by the intentions accompanying them. The Prophet, peace upon him, affirmed this in one of the axial hadiths, "Actions are only judged based on the intentions accompanying them."[215] There are no external factors that can corrupt our intention without our being complicit in facilitating that corruption. Hence, we are the only thing standing between ourselves and a pure intention. On the other hand, there are many external factors beyond our control that may render our actions themselves less than perfect.

We could mention in this regard, a lack of requisite knowledge, interruptions beyond our control, and a lack of qualified teachers. While we may spend a lifetime perfecting our actions, as we learn ever deeper levels of the divine law, our intention can potentially be in order from the minute we become conscious Muslims. Saying this does not mean that our intentions are not also amenable to improvement, they certainly are. However, a truthful and sincere person's intention will always be better than his or her actions.

Here in America we have a saying, "Actions speak louder than words." A truthful person's actions will always have a deeper and far more penetrating impact than his or her words. One reason is that he or she will try harder to demonstrate their sincerity with their actions more than they will with their words. They realize that actions and not words are the true measure of sincerity. Consistent with this meaning, those who lack sincerity will try to impress with their words, while their actions will oftentimes be totally inconsistent with their professions. Such people are condemned in the strongest terms in the Qur'an. God mentions, *O Believers! Why do you say that which you fail to do? Grievously hated is it with God that you say what you do not do.* (61:2)

A similar condemnation is found in the following verse, *Among people there is one whose speech in worldly affairs amazes you. He calls God to witness as to what is in his heart, while he is the most contentious disputant.* (2:204) The relevant point with such a person is that his actions are so incongruous with his speech that he is compelled to call God to witness as to what his true intentions are. However, his contentiousness and the corruption that ensues in his wake clearly reveal his lack of both sincerity and truthfulness.

His home is the truth.

A believer is at home with the truth because he has committed his life to it. He follows it steadfastly. Truth becomes ingrained into his very being. He seeks out the truthful and is comfortable with them. Because of his dedication to truth in this world, he is blessed with Paradise, which is an abode qualified by truth.

One of the names of Paradise is *Dar al-Salaam* or the Abode of Peace. One meaning of this is an abode where there will be no defects. One of the manifestations of the defectiveness of the world is the existence of lies. The defectiveness of lying is that it involves a lessening or corruption of the truth. In Paradise, this will not occur. Hence, the believer in Paradise will be at home with the truth.

His sanctuary is shyness.

Shyness is an integral part of our faith. The Prophet, peace upon him, stated, "Faith is seventy some odd branches, the highest of which is declaring, 'There is no god but God,' and the lowest of which is removing the harmful object from the pathway, and shyness is one of the branches of faith."[216] He also said, "Shyness only brings good."[217] It was said that the Prophet, peace upon him, was shyer than a virgin girl in the inner chamber of her house."[218]

The Prophet, peace upon him, once counseled a man, "You should be as shy before God as you would be in the presence of a man from the righteous elders of your people."[219] This particular hadith helps us to understand how shyness can be a sanctuary. When we are shy before God we are ashamed of violating His commandments and prohibitions. Our shyness keeps us in check. Therefore, it is a sanctuary from sin and rebellion against God, and consequently, against the associated punishment of Hell.

He is known for his impeccability in religion.

A truthful and sincere person does not seek shortcuts in his religious affairs. His sincerity pushes him to offer his very best to God. We should see our worship as service that we are offering God. When we engage in a half-hearted prayer, when we abandon voluntary acts that we could have easily completely, when we are lax in examining our intentions and we are not trying to perfect our actions, we are not being impeccable in our religion. Such traits or actions are far removed from the righteous.

God-consciousness is his witness. He has heart-vision rooted in the light of knowledge that allows him to truly see, to articulate deeper truths embedded in knowledge, and to give expression to proofs of certitude.

We have previously commented on all of the things mentioned in this passage. Here we wish to emphasize that this is the description of the religious person we are aspiring to become. Such people are special and constitute a proof for God. As we see ourselves immersed in the midst of an increasingly crass and vulgar popular culture that is encouraging people to forfeit their dignity, nobility, and religion, by embodying and then exemplifying these characteristics, we represent something special in the world.

During a time when the lack of worldly possessions was weighing on some of the wives of the Prophet, peace upon him, they were reminded by God, *O Wives of the Prophet! You are not like ordinary women.* (33:32) We should realize, especially at this time when the world needs a paradigm shift away from the destructive consumerist, objectifying mentality that threatens to destroy the natural environment that we are not like ordinary people. We should live our lives with purpose. Part of that purpose should be that we are consciously trying to present an alternative to the people of the world.

CHAPTER SIX

Only those who struggle against the base impulses of their souls, for the sake of God, attain to that station.

Attaining the lofty stations of human and spiritual excellence, which have been mentioned in the past few sections, is not an easy task. It requires a serious struggle. The beginning of that struggle has to be that it is undertaken for the sake of God. God mentions, *Those struggling for our sake, we will them guide in our paths.* (29:69) That struggle is difficult. Hence, it is referred to as a *Jihad.* This struggle is central in Islam, for it culminates in a pure intention, a rectified heart, and love of God.

He is consistently obedient.

Consistency is one of the most desirable aspects of our religion. The Prophet, peace upon him, stated, "The most beloved acts with God are those done most consistently."[220] Over time, those actions lead to our fully incorporating them, and more importantly, their fruits into the core of our being. This is the essence of uprightness in religion. This meaning is indicated by another hadith. The Prophet, peace upon him, was asked for guidance that was so concise yet clear and effective that it would need no subsequent clarification. He responded, peace upon him, "Declare, 'I believe in God!' and thereafter be consistently upright."[221]

Those who are familiar with the nuances of the Arabic language know that the particle conveying the meaning *thereafter,* "thumma," indicates the lapsing of a considerable period of time. In other words, consistent uprightness in religion does not occur in an instant, but only after the lapsing of a considerable period of time. It is here that consistency comes into play. One has to slowly but steadily build a reality of righteousness. If our spiritual transformation comes too suddenly, then in all likelihood it is neither real nor deep.

His intention is good.

One of the signs of a good intention is that a person is given consistency in his or her actions. Hence, a person that God blesses to achieve the descriptions that we are mentioning here has an intention that is pleasing to God. The description of the person possessing these qualities began with the mention of his sincerity and truthfulness. The essence of his or her sincerity is that he/she only seeks the pleasure of God in their lives and with their worship.

In this regard, sincerity is a function of the believer's truthfulness, for it is basically an expression of the believer's honesty in dealing with God. Such sincerity encompasses the depth of the believer's commitment to God, and his or her internalizing all of the meanings of the expression that serves as the buttress supporting all else in the religion, namely the declaration— There is no god but God (*La ilaha illa Allah*).

One of the greatest fruits of this sincerity is conveyed to us in the following hadith: The Prophet, peace upon him, said, "The person most likely to receive my intercession on the Day of Resurrection will be one saying with utmost sincerity from his heart, *La ilaha illa Allah!"* 222

He reverences God publicly and privately.

One of the signs of true faith is that it leads its possessor to manifest it wherever he or she may be because of the awareness that God has the ability to see, hear and witness us at all times. Hence, for the righteous there is no difference in their public and private behavior. One of the great tribulations befalling many people in our time is that they appear as saints in public, but in the privacy of their homes they are tyrants and oppressors. Such behavior is totally unacceptable and one behaving thus will be taken to task by God. The Prophet, peace upon him, has admonished us to be mindful of God, both publicly and privately.

One of his prayers was the following, "O God! I ask you to grant me reverence of You, privately and publicly."223 Imam al-Shafi'i mentioned, "The three most precious things are giving charity during times of need; being impeccably mindful of God in private; and speaking the truth in the face of one you hope to benefit from, or one you fear.224

He has cut short expectations [for a long life].

One of the greatest forms of deception in this world is the assumption that we will be given a long life. Hence, we assume that we have ample time to repent, ample time to get serious about the religion, ample time to restore broken relations. Oftentimes, our enjoyment of worldly delights and pleasures leads to our procrastination in undertaking good deeds.

Such thinking is deceptive because tomorrow is promised to no one. One of the reasons this fact escapes the procrastinator is his or her infatuation with the world. They revel in its delights and do not stop to take time to consider the sobering reality of death, which is one of the greatest means of cutting short one's hopes for a long life and ones procrastination in undertaking religious responsibilities.

In this respect, one of the most penetrating bits of advice ever given is contained in the saying of the Prophet, peace upon him, "Be in the world as if you are a stranger or a wayfarer." In the same hadith he mentioned, "When you turn in at night do not anticipate that you will live until the morning, and when you arise in the morning do not anticipate that you will live until the evening."[225]

He has "tightened the belt" of cautiousness.

Such a person is extremely cautious in his religion for he knows that salvation is at stake. The essence of caution in our religion is captured in the saying of one of the early Muslims, "Caution lies in leaving that which is lawful fearing that it will lead to the unlawful."[226] The motivation pushing a believer to cautiousness is his fear that he will fall into doubtful matters. Obviously, this is a higher station than leaving forbidden things.

For this reason, cautiousness, which I have referred to earlier in this commentary as impeccability, is described by the Prophet, peace upon him, as the best manifestation of true religion. He mentioned, "Excessive knowledge is more beloved to me than excessive worship, and the best manifestation of true religion lies in cautiousness."[227]

He has set sail with the winds of {God's} protection across the sea of pure devotion.

Once we understand that there is no refuge from God except to Him, it is easy to devote ourselves to Him. This is so because we understand that the key to His protection is through devotion to Him. Imam al-Muhasibi expresses that idea here in beautiful, poetic language. Perhaps the greatest fruit of pure devotion is willing obedience. This is a very important concept now because too many people live lives which seem to indicate their desire to have God devoted to them, on their terms. A manifestation of this perverse type of devotion is found in their desire to have God obey them by having His religion conform to their desires and tastes. Of course, that will not happen. Hence, in many instances such people end up abandoning religion.

His time is a source of benefit. His states are sound. He is not deceived by the adornment of the abode of deception nor distracted by the shimmering mirages of its enticing breezes from the horrors of the Day of Resurrection. He gains the victory of attaining the station of wakefulness after experiencing the sleep of heedlessness.

Once a person enters into the protection of God through strict devotion to Him, he is no longer vulnerable to the vicissitudes of the world, for God shields him from them. He is able to use his time wisely and is not distracted by all that the world throws at him by way of temptation and deception. Such a person realizes that he must inevitably stand before God and that he will be responsible for everything he did in the world. His awareness that this is his end helps him to keep his eye on the prize—the lasting home of the Hereafter.

The attainment of the heavenly home is contingent on a person awakening from the sleep of heedlessness in this world. This is one of the greatest fruits of the spiritual path, to be alert and awake in this world and therefore capable of avoiding the many snares and pitfalls that it contains. This is not an easy task. Success in such an endeavor requires full alertness.

The state of wakefulness referred to here is a state of the heart. It is a description of the heart's alertness and sensitivity to the commandments and prohibitions of God. At a higher level, it is an expression of the heart's constant state of remembrance of God. It is related by Jabir that a group of angels came to the Prophet, peace upon him, while he was sleeping. One of them said, "He is sleeping." Another rejoined, "Verily, the eye sleeps, but the heart sleeps not."[228]

You should know that when the knowledge of the intelligent person is sound and his certitude is firm he knows that nothing will save him from his Lord except truthfulness. He therefore strives diligently in its quest and searches for the characteristics of its people, longing to know true life before his death, in order to prepare for the abode of permanence after his passing. Therefore, he sells his soul and his wealth to his Lord having heard Him say, Verily, God has purchased from the believers their souls and their wealth and for that they will have Paradise. (9:111)

In this passage Imam al-Muhasibi summarizes many of the themes we have commented on thus far. We will focus on the Qur'anic verse at the end of the passage for it demonstrates the awesome magnanimity of God. We know that everything in His creation belongs to God. He mentions in the Qur'an, *Unto God belongs everything in the heavens and on Earth.* (2:284) Similarly, we proclaim when afflicted with a calamity, *We belong to God and unto Him we are returning.* (2:156) Likewise, *Give them from the wealth of God, which He has bestowed on you.* (24:33)

Despite the fact that God already owns our lives and our wealth, He purchases them back from us after having loaned them to us! There could be no greater expression of His generosity. Furthermore, in exchange He does not give us something light, insignificant or petty. He gives us Paradise, the greatest of all prizes, the most precious of all gifts.

No one should ever be depressed by his or her worldly situation as long as he or she is walking on the path leading to Paradise. Attaining Paradise is the great objective of this life, and the person who gains it is victorious, regardless of what he achieved in the world. God mentions, *Every soul will experience death, and then you will be given your recompense in full on the Day of Resurrection. Therefore, whoever is pulled back from Hell and entered into Paradise is the victorious one. And what is the life of this world except a deceptive enjoyment?* (3:185)

He now has knowledge after ignorance, he is enriched after being impoverished, he has conviviality after being estranged, he is drawn near after being distant, and he rests after being exhausted.

When one awakens and discovers the purpose of life, one begins to live a different reality. The stark contrast between a person's former and new reality is highlighted by the contrasts Imam al-Muhasibi mentions here. The knowledge, wealth, sociability, and peace the person who discovers his proper relationship with God experiences are realities that are rooted in the state of his heart and the maturation of his soul. That person's entire life is transformed. An example of a person who made such a transformation is the wife of the Aziz of Egypt, Zulaykha, whose affair is highlighted in the story of Joseph. Here was a woman who knew no inner peace and whose life was overwhelmed by her enslavement to her carnal lusts and appetites.

As a result she conspired by the vilest of means to seduce Joseph. When her lowly state was exposed she refused to take any responsibility for her actions, rather she sought to place all of the blame on Joseph. However, after she matured and moved away from her ignorance and lowliness, she could see in the light of truth that indeed she was to blame and she readily acknowledged her guilt. Just as the Qur'an records the actions she undertook when she was a lowly prisoner of her lusts, it records her lofty words after her transformation and spiritual maturation. We read, *The truth is now clear; I indeed tried to seduce him* (Joseph) *while he is among the truthful. I do not absolve myself of any blame. Verily, the undisciplined soul inclines towards vileness, except one my Lord bestows mercy on. Verily, my Lord is forgiving and merciful.* (12:51, 53)

His affair becomes harmonious, his concern becomes focused, God-consciousness becomes his symbol, and awareness of God's constant watch over him becomes his state. Have you not considered the saying of the Messenger of God, peace upon him, "Worship God as if you see Him, and if you fail to see Him be mindful that He watches over you."[229]

We have previously discussed these themes at length. Hence we leave the reader to reflect on their meaning here without comment. Imam al-Muhasibi proceeds to elaborate on the characteristics of the spiritually mature.

A stranger thinks that he is does not speak because he is a mute. However, it is his wisdom that has silenced him. An simple-minded person may think he is a chatterbox. However, his deep desire to give sincere advice for the sake of God has caused him to speak so much. One might think he is wealthy. However, his chaste refraining from

asking anything of people has enriched him. A person might consider him impoverished. However, humility has made him content with a lowly station.

The important point here is that a person of God graciously accepts God's decree. It is said, "Be where God places you." If God places his servant in a situation that calls for silence, he is silent. If He places him in a situation where he must speak, then he speaks. He is neither pretentious nor does he make claims to stations that God has not elevated him to.

Such a person is beautifully described by the Prophet, peace upon him, in the hadith, "Paradise is for a servant who seizes the reins of his steed in the way of God. His hair is disheveled and his feet dust-covered. If he is in the front of the army, he gives that its full right. If he is bringing up the rear, he gives that its full right."[230] This servant only desires to please God and he seeks any and every opportunity God gives him to do just that. If he is in the front of the army where the heroes will be known for their valor, he gives that its full right. If is in the rear of the army "mopping up," he gives that its full right.

He does not expose himself to those things that are of no concern to him. He does not burden himself with more than what suffices him. He does not take what he does not need, nor does he leave that which he has been entrusted to protect. People are comfortable with him, but he is hard on himself. He has killed his longing for worldly things with caution in religion. He has cut off his extraneous cravings with God-consciousness, and he has extinguished his carnal appetites with the light of knowledge.

The Prophet, peace upon him, said, "From a person's Islam being good is his leaving what does not concern him."[231] Our concern is the Hereafter, and the successful meeting with God. Our concern is working so that we can be amongst those experiencing the Beatific Vision. Whatever helps us towards these goals in this world we gladly engage in it. We leave all else.

Imam al-Muhasibi mentions here that such a person is easy on the people, but hard on himself. This is the way of people of true knowledge. They understand the vastness of the religion and attempt to guide people to enjoy the ease to be found in that vastness, never assuming that another person is capable of what they themselves can bear of strictness and impeccability in religious matters. This is consistent with the message of the Qur'an. God mentions, *We have made no difficulty for you in your religion.* (22:78) *God desires ease for you. He desires no difficulty.* (2:185)

When informed that a man who was afflicted with a head injury had died when he was instructed to take a full cleansing bath, after experiencing a wet dream, in lieu of the symbolic purification with dry earth (*Tayammum*), the Prophet, peace upon him, repeatedly stated, "They have killed him! May God punish them!" He then said, "Why did they not ask if they did not know the ruling? Surely, inquiry is the cure for ignorance."[232]

We should understand that our religion is predicated on ease. If we are inspired to pursue a stricter course in our religious affairs then that is laudable. However, we should look deeply into the states of people and leave them where God has placed them. If we fail to do so, we could well undermine their religious progress, or turn them away from religion altogether.

Thus should you be. People like them are the one's you should associate with; and it is their way you should follow. Adopt their character. Such people are a preserved treasure. Anyone who sells them for some worldly gain has cheated himself.

All of the lessons and guidance that has been presented in these pages is not for entertainment, nor is it an empty academic exercise. It is to be implemented in our lives. The way of the people described here is the way we should endeavor to live. The Prophet Muhammad, peace upon him, is described in the Qur'an as a most excellent example. *Surely, you have in the Messenger of God a most excellent example for anyone who looks forward to meeting God, the Last Day, and remembers God much.* (33:21)

The scholars are the heirs of the Prophet, peace upon him. If we want to follow his way, we must follow the righteous among them. If we want to assimilate his state, we must keep the company of the pious among them. This is critical to our salvation. Ibn 'Ajiba, expresses this truth in these terms, "I swear by God! No one has succeeded of those who have succeeded except through the companionship of those who have succeeded."[233]

They are a source of support during tribulations and those who will be there to protect you amongst your friends. When you are impoverished they enrich you. When they pray to God they do not neglect you, They are the Party of God. Surely the Party of God is successful. (58:22)

A true friend is a friend whose companionship is established for the sake of God. The Prophet, peace upon him, mentioned among the seven categories of people who will be shaded by the Throne of God on the Day of Judgment will be two people who loved each other for the sake of God.[234] When friendship is established through God it is not qualified nor can it be affected by worldly motivations. Such friends are a source of support and enrichment for you, especially spiritual enrichment. One of the ways they enrich you is by praying for you when you are not present. They do not neglect you in this respect.

This particular prayer is especially powerful. The Prophet, peace upon him, said, "The prayer for a Muslim for his brother in his absence is answered. Near his head is an assigned angel. Every time he prays for his brother he says, "Amin. You will have the same."[235]

These are the people representing God's religion on earth. Hence, they are deservingly known as the Party of God. Success will be theirs, and success will be for those they pray for. If we think that we know one of them we should try to remember to pray for him.

You should know, may God expand our hearts, illuminate them with knowledge, and focus our concern through certitude, that the source of every tribulation that enters the heart is a consequence of excessiveness. The source of such excessiveness is becoming involved in worldly entanglements while in a state of ignorance and forgetting the return to God after gaining knowledge. The cure for that state is leaving involvement with anything whose ruling you are ignorant of, owing to impeccable religious practice, and only engaging in known things based on certainty.

Excessiveness is the source of much spiritual harm. When God created this world He established a balance. He has admonished us that we do not disrupt that balance. We read in the Qur'an, *The All Merciful! He has taught the Qur'an, He has created the human being. He has taught him elocution. The sun and moon follow determined courses. The stars and trees are in prostration. He has raised the heavens and established the balance; that you do not disrupt the balance.* (55:1-8)

As believers we are warned against excessiveness because it is excessiveness that disrupts the balance. Ibrahim al-Nakha'i, one of the most learned scholars of the early generations of Islam, said: "Rather those ruined before you were ruined owing to three characteristics: Excessive talking, excessive eating; and excessive sleeping."[236] It is interesting to note that the Fast of Ramadan helps to eliminate all of these sources of excess. Naturally, we eat less, if we are fasting properly. We speak less if we are cognizant of the etiquettes associated with the fast; such as the saying of the Prophet, peace upon him, "One who does not leave false speech and acting on it, God has no need for him to leave his food and drink."[237]

Finally, owing to arising early to partake of the pre-dawn meal, and to turning in to bed later due to the special Ramadan prayers, we sleep less. One of the surest means to avoid dangerous entanglement with the world is by knowing the ruling of the divine law in everything you do in this world. For example, ask yourself before purchasing something, "Is this transaction lawful?" If we proceed in this manner, we will build our affair on certitude and clear knowledge. This is one of the keys to a successful religious life.

I have found that the corruption of the heart leads to the corruption of religion. Have you not considered the saying of the Messenger of God, "Surely in the body is an organ, if it is sound the entire body is sound and if it is corrupt the entire body is corrupt, surely it is the heart."[238] The meaning of the heart[239] here is the religion, for it is religion that determines the soundness or corruption of the limbs.

This prophetic hadith has particularly profound implications. We know that the physical body cannot be healthy without a healthy heart. If the heart is diseased or weak and its ability to pump blood throughout the body is compromised then multiple problems will ensue. Poor blood circulation leads to a wide array of maladies, many of which are ruinous to the extremities.

Such is the case in religion. If the heart is corrupt it orders the limbs to engage in unacceptable actions: The tongue will lie, or eat of the forbidden; the eyes will gaze upon forbidden things; the ears will listen to corrupting words or music; the hands will steal, usurp, or murder; and the feet will convey one to places of iniquity, sin, and debauchery.

This parable can be extended even further. The man is the heart of the family, if he is corrupt then the family will likely be corrupt. If he permits his wife to display her body in unseemly ways, to come and go as she pleases, to associate with a seedy ilk of people whose values are corrupt, her character will likely reflect realities that are ruinous to the family at large. If he does not endeavor to discipline his children, or guard what they watch on television, to censor the music they listen to, or monitor their friends and associations, then these things will help to undermine the health and integrity of his family. Similarly, the king, president, or leader of a nation is an exemplar for his or her subjects. If he lies, cheats, steals, plunders the public treasury, engages in policies that display blatant nepotism, or whose benefits accrue to a small circle of ideological allies, and does not work to ensure that civility and respect for the rule of law prevail in the public square, then his actions will likely have a ruinous effect on society at large.

The source of the heart's corruption is failing to take account of the soul and being deceived into expecting a long life. Therefore, if you want to rectify your heart take time to question your desires and thoughts. Engage in those things that are strictly undertaken for the pleasure of God and leave everything else. Help yourself to conquer the expectation of longevity by constantly remembering death.

The remembrance of death is one of the greatest sources of rectification for an errant heart. It is extremely difficult to remain spiritually sober if one does not remember death frequently. An Arab poet mentioned:

> O My companion! Be serious and constantly
> remember death,
> for its neglect is a source of clear straying."[240]

God mentions in the Qur'an, *Every soul will taste of death, and you will be given your recompense in full on the Day of Resurrection...* (3:185) The Prophet, peace upon, said, "The intelligent person is one who regularly takes himself to account, and works for what will come after his death."[241] He also said, "Be in the world as if you are a stranger or a wayfarer and consider yourself among the people already in their graves."[242] These narrations remind us that death is an inescapable reality.

Despite that, many people are in abject denial concerning death. They try to deny it in a number of ways. Some do it through the quest for eternal youth. Some do it through acquisitiveness. Some do it through an insatiable quest for

power. Some do it through various other forms of megaloma-
nia. However, death will inevitably come to each and every
one of us. Then the realities many people denied, especially
those relating to the torment of the grave and accountability
before God, will be made clear to them. It is mentioned in the
Qur'an, *Your mutual rivalry in piling up distracts you, until you
visit the graves.* (102:1-2)

We should not wait until we are in our graves to realize
the seriousness of death and the after-life. We should begin
now. We should take time to reflect on a time this life will
leave us. We should reflect on lying in our graves surrounded
by dirt and silence. We should take time to reflect on how
we will respond to the questioning of the angels, *Munkar* and
Nakir. We should be especially cognizant of the fact that there
is no running away from death. God mentions in the Qur'an,
*Say, the death that you are fleeing from will surely meet you. Then,
you will be returned to the knower of all things, both hidden and
manifest, and He will inform you of all that you did.* (62:8)

**I have found that the sources of the varying types of
excessiveness that affect the heart manifest themselves
in hearing, sight, speech, food, clothing, and houses.**

Excess is an inevitable consequence of a capitalist society. With all aspects of life reduced to commodities, more of
everything means more money for those who have commod-
itized our world. This leads to more things to listen to. The
more we listen, the more music we will buy, or the more we
will buy of commodities whose sale is tied to advertisements
that skillfully use music to get us into the mood to "shop
until we drop."

This condition leads to more things to see as our eyesight
is bombarded again with the products that are consciously
placed in a position to stimulate our vision with maximum

effect. The same can be said for speech. Think of how much the advent of cell phones alone has increased the volume of our speech.

The commoditizing of our food clearly leads to excess. The more food we can sell the more money we make. Why should we be content selling people six-once increments of a particular beverage if we can sell them a forty-eight once "Big Gulp?" Why encourage them to be content with a quarter pound of beef on their sandwich if we can sell them a "half-pounder?" Why be content to sell them a liter of water daily if we can convince them their skin will only remain supple if they drink one-tenth of their bodyweight in water every day?

The same goes for clothing and homes. We are inundated with constantly expanding artificial needs. We need to refresh our wardrobes four times a year to ensure that we have the proper clothing for the proper season. Although we are a single couple with a small infant it is unthinkable that we would purchase a house with less than three bathrooms. It is related that the Prophet, peace upon him, could not stand erect in his house, yet we need "cathedral" ceilings in our homes. All of this material excessiveness and acquisitiveness is destroying this planet by raping the earth of her finite resources and by creating an ever mounting crisis of waste disposal. As Muslims, we should be people who are moderate in what we consume, conscious of the example we may set for the present and future generations.

Excessive hearing leads to forgetfulness and heedlessness.

As our senses are inundated with music—in the home, the store, the car, the shop or office—we forget about God, for it is only through His remembrance that we remain mindful of Him. This leads to heedlessness as it only through God-consciousness that we are able to be mindful of His commandments and prohibitions.

In a state of heedlessness we forget about His commandments and prohibitions. However, our heedlessness will not endure forever. One day we will be painfully reminded of our reckless irresponsibility. God says, *He (God) will say, Thus it was that when our signs came to you, you forgot them. Hence, on this day you will be forgotten.* (20:126)

Excessive sight leads to heedlessness and confusion.

As our sight is bombarded with an ever increasing array of images, our minds are required to process them. As our minds conflate some images with others, oftentimes images conveying contradictory messages, confusion is the inevitable result. Such confusion only serves to intensify our heedlessness, as God becomes increasingly abstract to us, until we can not even conceive of Him in a meaningful way.

Excessive speech leads to empty chattering and heretical utterances.

The more we talk, the greater the likelihood that much of our talk will be void of any significant messages. We also run the risk of saying things that involve heresy or blasphemy, because we are subtly conditioning ourselves not to monitor our speech. One of the characteristics of the believers is that they avoid empty, unproductive talk. God mentions in the Qur'an, *The believers are indeed successful; those who are humble in their prayers and those who avoid empty talk.* (23:1-2)

Excessive food leads to greed and artificial needs.

The more we eat, the more we feel we have to eat. We condition ourselves to need food because a particular time has been designated for eating and not because we are hungry. We tell ourselves, it is breakfast, eat! It is ten o'clock snack break, eat! It is lunch time, eat! It is afternoon snack time, eat! It is dinner time, eat! It is midnight snack time, eat! This schedule only institutionalizes a series of artificial needs and cements our essential greed.

Islam encourages seeing reality for what it is. This includes our needs. We should see them for what they really are. If we are not hungry at a particular time then we should not eat. If we do not need to hop into the car to take the children four blocks to school we should not do it. If we do not need a larger house, we should not buy one. Only by deeply assessing the reality of our situation will we be able to make the deep changes we need to make to become a more viable and relevant community.

Excessive clothing leads to boasting and ostentatious behavior.

This is the essence of the idea of fashion. To show off the unique and distinctive garments we possess vis-à-vis other people. We can all involve ourselves in this game if we choose to do so. However, at the end of the day, the root of such behavior is boastfulness and ostentation. One obsessed with clothing should be warned by the following words of the Prophet, peace upon him. He said, "Ruined is the worshipper of clothing."[243]

One of the symbols of arrogance and ostentation in the Qur'an is Qarun. Consider one of his attributes, *So he went out before his people in all of his finery...* (28:79) Some Qur'an commentators explain that among his *finery* was gold and silk clothing. His insecurity, his distance from God, and his slavery to his base desires pushed him to seek a sense of purpose and importance in vainglorious, self-aggrandizing behavior.

Excessively large houses lead to waste and conceit.

Excessively large homes are a waste of space and a waste of resources. When we engage in such waste just to be able to say, "This is my house, and it is the biggest on the block," we are engaging in a fool's game that not only threatens the planet, it threatens our very souls. Sufficient warning for us in that regard is the description God gives of wasteful people in the Qur'an. He says, *Wasteful folk are the brothers of Satan, and Satan is ungrateful to his Lord.* (18:27)

It is one thing to lawfully enjoy the blessings that God gives one. It is quite another to plunder the earth's resources in a lifestyle that defies logical explanation in terms of its wastefulness and lack of consideration for the ecological limitations of the planet and the inability of others to meet even their most basic needs. Our religion is calling us to a higher ethical standard. We have to all challenge ourselves in order to rise up to that standard.

CHAPTER SEVEN

You should know that protecting the limbs is an obligation, while abandoning excessiveness is a highly desired virtue.

Protecting our limbs from rebellion against God and hence from the Hellfire is a binding obligation. God mentions in the Qur'an, *Do not allow your hands to contribute to your destruction.* (2:195) Although this expression is said to have been revealed in the context of withholding support for the armed defense of the community, and hence facilitating the ability of the enemies of Islam to vanquish the Muslim community, it has a general meaning. By refusing to spend, as we have been mandated to do by God, we allow our hands to rebel against God and thereby expose our souls to divine punishment and retribution. This is true in all acts that involve the sins of our extremities.

Repentance before all of that is an obligation. This is an obligation imposed by God and His Messenger. God, Majestic is His remembrance, says, O Believers! Repent sincerely to God. (66:8) The meaning of sincerity is the servant not returning to what he has repented to his Lord for. The Messenger of God, peace upon him, said, "O People! Repent to your Lord before you die, and draw yourself near to Him with righteous deeds before you become preoccupied."[244]

Repentance is the beginning of the spiritual path. Its discussion is the first topic that Imam Ghazali deals with in the section of *The Revival of the Religious Sciences* that details those things necessary for salvation. He mentions:

> Surely repentance from sinning, by returning to the one who conceals faults and knows the unseen, is the beginning of the path for those seeking to travel to God. It is the capital of those who are successful in life. It is the first step for those desiring spiritual elevation. It is the key for the rectification of those inclining towards sin, and it is the point of departure for the purification and selection of those destined to be close to God.[245]

It is through our repentance that we communicate to God the seriousness of our quest for change, and, eventually salvation. If we remain on the reckless path that is leading us to perdition, if we maintain the bad habits that involve rebellion against God and His Messenger, if we do not take the time try to set in order the house we have destroyed before endeavoring to build another house, what message are we sending? God mentions in the Qur'an, *One who rejects the false deity and then believes in God has gasped a firm handhold that will never break.* (2:256)

This verse expresses a process that is foundational in the spiritual quest, emptying out (*takhliya*) and then adorning (*tahliya*). We clean and sand the old walls before we paint them. We sweep or vacuum the dirt from the floor and wash it before we put down a new carpet. Similarly, we rid ourselves of our bad habits before we adorn ourselves with positive and virtuous characteristics and behaviors.

Repentance is not proper unless it involves four things: A conviction not to return {to the sinful behavior}; a request for forgiveness coupled with remorse; the usurped property or rights are returned or restored to the aggrieved party; and the limbs are protected from the potentially corrupting influence of the seven senses, namely: hearing, sight, speech, smell, the two hands, the two feet, and the heart, which is the commander of the others. With it lies the rectitude or ruin of the body.

This passage emphasizes how important it is for us to work for the purification and the rectification of our hearts. As has been previously mentioned, the heart is the commander of the body. The body will follow it in uprightness or in profligacy. Ibn Rajab al-Hanbali states:

> There is no rectification for the heart until gnosis is firmly established in it, along with the exaltation of God, His love, His reverence, appreciation of His awesomeness, hoping for His mercy, total reliance on Him, and then the heart being filled with those qualities. This is real monotheism. This is the meaning of "There is no god but God." [246]

We cannot overemphasize how important the rectification of the heart is. Our success in this world depends on it, as does our salvation in the next. God describes the Day of Judgment as, *A day when neither wealth nor children will be of any benefit, except for one coming before God with a rectified heart.* (26:88-89)

One of the fervent prayers of the Prophet, peace upon, was, "O God! I ask you for a rectified heart."[247]

God has created for each limb a command and a prohibition as a binding obligation. He has created between these two a space for permissible actions. Leaving that space is a laudable virtue for the servant.

As individuals we are religiously responsible. That religious responsibility also includes the charity we owe for every bone in our bodies. God has a right over them just as He has a right over us. This idea is affirmed by the Prophet, peace upon him. He said, "Every bone in the human body has the duty upon it to give charity with each rising sun."[248] The responsible person pays this charity on behalf of his body.

The origin of this charity arises from the tremendous blessing we have been given from our Lord through the miraculous body He has blessed us with. The charity owed for it is an expression of our appreciation for this blessing. We can convey that appreciation in several ways. One of them is mentioned in the following hadith:

> Whoever says at the time of awakening in the morning, "Whatever blessing You have bestowed upon me or upon any human, it is from You, You are alone without partners. Unto You is all praise and unto You is all thanks," has conveyed the appreciation due from him that day. And whoever says it in the evening has conveyed the thanks due that night.[249]

The obligation of the heart, after faith and repentance, is being sincere in the actions undertaken for the sake of God; entertaining a good opinion of God during those situations that vex your understanding; trusting

in His promise; fearing His punishment; and hoping for His grace.

Here, several rights owed to God are mentioned. Faith is an affirmation of His exclusive right to worship (*ilahiyya*) for we are expressing our belief in Him as it is a right owed to Him that we believe. Repentance is an affirmation of His lordship (*rububiyya*) for we are acknowledging that He has the power to act in His creation, and that His power is not confined to a material calculus. Among His exclusive power is the power to forgive our sins and to obliterate their traces and effects.

After that we are enjoined to be sincere in our dealing with God. He is the one who has created us, blessed us with this life, created the means for us to learn, and to grow intellectually, and guided us to faith. At the end of our affair, it is He who will determine if we will spend eternity in Heaven or Hell. Who then could be more deserving of sincerity from us than God?

Imam al-Muhasibi then mentions having a good opinion of God. This is extremely important as God will manifest Himself to us in the way we think of Him. He says in a divine hadith, "I am as my servant thinks of Me."[250] If we think that God is gracious and generous, His grace and generosity will be manifested in our lives. If we think He is other than that, then that is what we will see manifested in our lives. Imam Shawkani mentions in this regard:

> This is an encouragement from God to His servants that they have a good opinion of Him, for He will treat them based on their opinion of Him. One who has a good opinion of Him will find the copious abundance of His goodness deluging him. He will send down on him the beauty of His graces,

shower him with the beautiful manifestations of His generosity, and bestow upon him unprecedented gifts.[251]

Here, Imam al-Muhasibi also reemphasizes just how important it is for us to trust, fear, and hope in God.

Various narrations have been related that give us insight into the heart. Among them is the saying of the Messenger of God, peace upon him, "Verily, amongst the believers are individuals my heart softens towards."[252]

Our hearts respond differently to different people. There are people that we instinctively find repulsive and there are others we have a great receptivity towards. One reason for this is the nature of the interaction of our souls with other souls in the pre-temporal realm before entering this world. This process is described by the Messenger of God, peace upon him, in the following hadith, "The souls are assembled hosts, those that recognize each other find harmony, while those that are unfamiliar with each other find dissonance."[253]

Ibn Hajar al-Asqalani mentions in *Fath al-Bari* that Imam al-Khattabi understood this to mean two things: People's souls are naturally disposed towards good or evil and when they meet those souls that are similarly inclined they gravitate towards each other, the good souls toward the good, the evil souls towards the evil. Another meaning he suggests is that it refers to the creation of the souls in the unseen world before they were united with their bodies in the visible world. Some souls met and found a harmonious attraction towards each other in the unseen world, while others found dissonance, while yet others never have met. Once they enter their respective bodies and then meet in this world they respond to each other based on their prior responses in the unseen realm.[254] This is the reason some of us can meet a person for the first time and sense we have known them all of our lives. Unbeknown to most of us, we actually have.

He also said, peace upon him, "Verily, truth comes emanating light, it is thus incumbent upon you to guard the inner sanctums of the heart."[255]

The origin of this hadith is unknown. It could have possibly been recorded in one of the millions of volumes that were lost during the sacking of Baghdad at the hands of the marauding Mongol Hordes. God knows best. In any case, the association of truth with light is nothing new or strange. Religious knowledge is truth. Some exegetes mention, concerning the expression ...and *they counsel each other with truth* (102:3) as meaning they counsel each other with the Qur'an.[256] The Prophet, peace upon him, said, "The Book of God contains guidance and light. Whoever holds tight to it will be guided, and whoever neglects it will go astray."[257] This is one meaning of the truth coming emanating light. The Qur'an is an embodiment of truth and it is a light. Another meaning is based on the fact that God is truth (*al-Haqq*), and He is also light (*al-Nur*). When He manifests Himself through His names, attributes, and actions, the truth comes emanating light.

The attainment of light is one the themes of our religion that is oftentimes lost. Perhaps the greatest expression of this theme is found in the following prophetic prayer, "O God! Place light in my heart, in my vision, and in my hearing. Place light on my right and on my left. Place light above me, beneath me, before me and behind me. O God! Magnify me with light."[258]

It is important to guard the inner sanctums of our hearts because they are the locus of the light mentioned in these narrations. If the heart is allowed to crust over as a consequence of sin and rebellion that light is unable to enter its inner sanctum. At this point, a person's guidance is not possible for there is no light to illuminate his path through the world.

Ibn Mas'ud mentioned: "The hearts have times when they are amenable to worship, and other times when they are languid. Take advantage of the times of amenability, and avoid the times of languidness."

[Abdullah] bin Mubarak mentioned, "The heart is like a mirror, if it is left sitting in your hand it will rust. It is also like a domesticated animal, if it is neglected by its owner it will become enfeebled."

We have to diligently monitor our hearts, take care of and properly nourish them. We should take advantage of the times our hearts incline towards certain actions by enthusiastically undertaking those particular acts. This is a way of maximizing our time, for when our hearts are inclined towards an act we will be capable of doing more of that particular action with enhanced focus and attentiveness.

If our hearts are not inclined towards an act we will perform less of it with decreased vigor and focus. In this case, it may sometimes be better to temporarily leave the act until our hearts are in a better state, or perform another act that our heart is receptive towards, seeking a greater reward through that act. We may actually undertake an act and receive little or no reward from God. This is so because the languidness of our heart might lead to us not even being aware of performing the action. God advises us in this regard, *Recite what is easy for you of the Qur'an.* (73:20)

One of the best ways of properly caring for our hearts is through the remembrance of God. God mentions in the

Qur'an, *Those who believe and their hearts find comfort in the remembrance of God. Surely, it is the remembrance of God that brings comfort to the hearts.* (13:28) Another very important way of caring for our hearts is by limiting the corrupting influences that can assail it. This is an issue Imam al-Muhasibi now takes up in great detail.

One of the sages said, "The heart is like a house with six doors. You are warned, 'Do not allow anyone to enter any of the doors lest they ransack your house!' The heart is the house, and the six doors are speech, vision, hearing, smell, the two hands and the two feet. Whenever any of these doors are breeched the house is pillaged."

The obligation governing speech is being truthful during times of pleasure or anger, refraining from harming others secretly or openly, and avoiding ostentatious speech, whether it is good or evil. The Messenger of God, peace upon him, mentioned, "Whoever will guarantee me that he will control what is between his two lips[259] and his two thighs, I will guarantee him Paradise."[260]

The Messenger of God, peace upon him, mentioned to Mu'adh bin Jabal, "Are people thrown into Hell and then dragged on their faces for anything other than the harvest of their tongues?"[261]

We should be especially mindful of the harvest of our tongues. Every word we utter is like a seed. At some time, sooner or later, our words will germinate, flower, and then yield a harvest. That harvest will be either a blessing or a curse, a source of joy or remorse. The Prophet, peace upon him, said, "A servant will speak a word not fully realizing its implications. For that word he slips into Hell deeper that the distance between the east and the west."[262]

Nothing is more ruinous to the successful salvation of the human than his or her tongue. Here, we will mention some of the ruinations of the tongue in order that we can take the proper measures to avoid them. This list is taken from Imam al-Ghazali's, *The Revival of the Religious Sciences*:

1. Speech in those areas of no relevance to the speaker.
2. Excessive speech.
3. Perverse speech.
4. Unconstructive arguing and disputation.
5. Verbal wrangling.
6. Pretentious speech.
7. Vile and abusive speech.
8. Invoking curses.
9. Lewd singing and poetry.
10. Excessive joking.
11. Sarcasm and ridicule.
12. Unjustifiably revealing secrets.
13. False promises.
14. Lying.
15. Backbiting
16. Scandal mongering.
17. Intentionally duplicitous speech.
18. Unconstructive praise.
19. Heedlessness concerning misleading details contained in one's speech.
20. Asking common people about intricate theological matters.[263]

Avoiding these ruinations is one of the greatest things we can do to help ward off the torment of Hell. The following two narrations, mentioned by Imam al-Muhasibi, reinforce this point.

The Prophet, peace upon him, said, "I warn you against excessive speech. What meets your needs suffices you. Surely, a man will be asked about his excessive speech just as he will be asked about his excessive wealth."[264] The Prophet, peace upon him, mentioned, "God is present at the tongue of every speaker. Therefore, let a person be mindful of God and know well everything he utters."[265]

We must be extremely diligent in guarding our speech. As we have mentioned, nothing can ruin a servant as rapidly or as thoroughly as his speech. The general ruling for the tongue is silence. As is the case in all affairs, we do not move away from a general ruling except for a religiously countenanced interest. Hence, if there is no interest to be advanced by our speaking, we should remain silent.

The obligation of the sight is that it is averted from gazing at something forbidden, and that it does not seek out what is veiled or hidden from it.

The Messenger of God, peace upon him, said, "The forbidden glance is one of Satan's arrows. Whoever abandons it motivated by the fear of God, God will grant him a level of faith whose sweetness he will find in his heart."[266]

Abu Darda' said, "Whoever avoids the forbidden gaze, God will wed him to any of the wide-eyed maidens of Paradise that he chooses; and whoever peeks from

rooftops, God will render him blind on the Day of
Resurrection."

Controlling the gaze is one of the distinctions of a believer. We are people of discipline and dignity. One of the signs of
people who have fallen into profligacy is their lustfully staring
at people in public spaces, or privately peeking into the sacred
spaces of other human beings. We defile our eyes when we use
them for these and other less than noble purposes.

We should be mindful of the fact that the eyes can engage in a type of fornication. The Prophet said in that regard,
"God has ordained that every human being would have his or
her share of fornication, which will inevitably be his lot. The
fornication of the eyes is the unlawful glance. The fornication of the tongue is the enticing word, while the soul longs
and lusts. The private parts then either confirm or belie those
precursors."[267]

We should all endeavor to be mindful of the wonderful
tidings given to our eyes and hence our very souls by the Messenger of God, peace upon him, when he said, "There are two
types of eyes that will not be touched by the Hellfire: An eye
that sheds tears out of reverence for God; and an eye that loses
sleep standing guard in the Way of God."[268] It is sometimes
overlooked that the greatest delight in Paradise, the Beatific
Vision, is a delight that is reserved for the eyes. God states
in the Qur'an, *Some faces will be illuminated that day, gazing
towards their Lord.* (75:22)

The Prophet, peace upon him, was known to pray, "Bless
me to gaze upon those things that will elicit Your pleasure
with me."[269] This is a beautiful prayer that should be always
on our tongues and present in our hearts.

These narrations affirm the sanctity of privacy, which is
a fundamental human right. God warns in the Qur'an, *Do
not spy on one another.* (49:12) This spying could be in a politi-

cal or a social sense. The inner sanctums of people's homes, their gatherings, and their correspondence are all sanctified and must be guarded. Privacy is valued to such a degree that a person who injures the eyes of one peeking through his window is not legally responsible for the offending party's injury or loss.

Dawud al-Ta'i said to a man who was glaring back at someone staring at him, "Avert your gaze, for it has reached me that a man will be asked about his superfluous glance just as he will be asked about his superfluous actions."

It is said, "The unintended forbidden glance is not held against the servant, this is not so for the subsequent glance."[270] Hence, the servant's untended forbidden glance is pardoned; this is not the case for what is premeditated. He is taken to account for that.

This is a general principle in our religion. We are only taken to task for those transgressions that we intentionally involve ourselves in. The unintentional glance which occurs spontaneously is beyond our control. Therefore, we are not taken to task for it. However, there was a time when the Companions of the Prophet, peace upon him, thought that they would be held accountable for even those actions they could not consciously control.

Imam Ahmad, Imam Muslim and others relate on the authority of Abu Hurayra that when the verse, *Whether you hide or reveal what is in your hearts, you will be taken to account for it by God.* (2:285) was revealed, it weighed heavily on the Companions. They went to the Messenger of God, peace upon him, fell down on their knees and said, "This verse has been revealed to you and we cannot bear its implications." He said,

"Do you desire to speak the words of those given the two books prior to you, "We hear and we disobey!" Rather say, "We hear and we obey. Forgiveness is yours our Lord and unto you is the return.""

As soon as they had recited this, God immediately revealed, *The Messenger believes in what has been revealed from his Lord as do the believers. Each believes in God, His Angels, His Scriptures, and His Messengers. We make no distinctions between the various Messengers. They say, "We hear and we obey, forgiveness is yours our Lord and unto you is the return."* (2:285) After they had recited that verse, the ruling of the earlier verse, *Whether you hide or reveal what is in your hearts, you will be taken to account for it by God,* was abrogated when God subsequently revealed, *God does not burden any soul beyond its capacity...* (2:286)[271] Mercifully, God informed them that they were not accountable for that beyond their control.

The obligation of the hearing is consistent with that of the speech and sight. Everything prohibited for you to speak about or to look at is prohibited for you to listen to or to enjoy audibly.

God mentions in the Qur'an, *Surely, the hearing, sight and the heart each will be asked about.* (17:36) In this verse, we are enjoined to use our God-given faculties wisely. We have to take every possible measure to ensure that we guard against evil in all of its manifestations. We should not listen to lewd and provocative speech or music. We should not look at indecent scenes, or images. We should not entertain vile and degrading thoughts, ideas and concepts. We will have to answer to God for all of these actions if we are guilty of them.

Another meaning of this verse is that each of our faculties will be asked about us. In other words, just as we will be asked about how we used our faculties, our faculties will be asked about how they were used. This should not be a far-fetched idea to anyone familiar with the Qur'anic message. We read, *On a day their tongues, hands and feet will bear witness against them for what they used to do.* (24:24)

We also know on the Day of Judgment the earth will be given the ability to speak and each place will testify as to the good or evil that occurred at its location. We read in the Qur'an, *On that day she will articulate her news, because her Lord has so inspired her.* (99:4-5) The Prophet, peace upon him, asked a group of his Companions, after reciting the above-mentioned verse, "Do you know what her news is?" They replied, "God and His Messenger know best." He said, "Her news is that she will bear witness for or against every servant, male and female, regarding what they did on her surface. She will say, 'On such and such day he/she did so and so.' This is her news."[272]

Searching for what is hidden from you is unlawful spying. Listening to empty amusement, sensuous singing, and words harming Muslims in any way is as forbidden as consuming carrion or blood. Ibn 'Umar said, "We were forbidden to either backbite or listen to it, or to carry tales between people or listen to them."

The themes introduced in this paragraph are powerfully summed up in a single verse in the Qur'an. God mentions, *O Believers! Avoid suspicion to the extent possible, for sometimes suspicion amounts to sin. Neither spy on nor backbite one another. Would one of you wish to eat the flesh of his dead brother? Surely, this would be something you would hate. Fear God, for surely God accepts repentance, and is most merciful.* (49:12)

When Imam al-Muhasibi mentions in this passage that harming a Muslim in any way is forbidden like consuming carrion or blood, he is reminding us of the sanctified nature of a Muslim. The Prophet mentioned in the context of a lengthier narration delineating the foundations of brotherhood in Islam, "Every Muslim is sacred to his fellow Muslim, his life, property and honor."[273]

Engaging in any activity that harms a Muslim is as prohibited as drinking alcohol or eating carrion or swine. We oftentimes miss this point. Sadly, in our day of anonymous electronic communications, we see Muslims harming each other in the most egregious ways via their computer keyboards. We even see websites or blogs set up to defile Muslims of upright character and exemplary service to the Ummah. Muslims who engage in such activity should think well before unleashing their fingers.

Qasim bin Muhammad bin Abu Bakr was asked about sensuous singing and he replied, "When God separates between truth and falsehood on the Day of Resurrection, where will sensuous singing end up?" It was said, "With falsehood." He then said, "Then seek a verdict from yourself."

Qasim bin Muhammad bin Abu Bakr was among a group of scholars of the generation that succeeded the Companions of the Prophet, peace upon him. They were known as the "Seven Jurists of Medina." Their ranks included Sa'id bin al-Musayyab, 'Urwa bin al-Zubayr, Abu Bakr bin 'Abdul Rahman bin al-Harith, 'Ubayd bin 'Abdullah bin 'Utbah bin Mas'ud, Kharija bin Zayd bin Thabit, and Sulayman bin Yasar. They were instrumental in the early formulation of the legal schools of Islam. In this quote from Qasim bin Muhammad, Imam al-Muhasibi is warning us against the danger of songs with vile lyrics and unacceptable instruments.

One of the most corrupting influences in modern societies is music. Popular songs contain lyrics that openly encourage fornication, adultery, prostitution, vile and thuggish behavior, drug and alcohol consumption, devil worship and a plethora of other vices. As Muslims we should be in the forefront of efforts to turn back this scourge, which is rooted in the sinister exploitation of people's lower desires for huge profits.

If we move beyond the overtly corrupting messages of such music, we find that most of our young people have been reduced to music consumers who spend countless hours listening to music—with no consideration as to the nature of the message. This destructive pattern of consumption wastes valuable time that could be used learning and memorizing the Qur'an, studying other aspects of sacred knowledge, arming oneself with the knowledge needed to help the Muslims compete in the modern world, or doing some constructive good for humanity at large.

We have previously mentioned the hadith,[274] "There are two blessings that most people are cheated out of: their health and their spare time."[275] In our society there is nothing that cheats people out of their spare time like music, with the exception of television.

There is no appendage more damaging to the servant, after his tongue, than his ears, because they are the fastest messenger to the heart, and the quickest to surrender to temptation. It has been related from Waki' bin Jarrah, "I heard something from an innovator twenty years ago, and I have not yet been able to expel it from my ears." Whenever an innovator came to Tawus he would cover his ears to avoid hearing his speech.

Imam al-Muhasibi here is reminding us that the faculties are conduits to our hearts and that we must protect what enters into those conduits if we are to protect our hearts. God mentions in the Qur'an, in the context of the corruption of those following Moses, *They said we hear but we disobey, and their hearts became filled with the love of the calf—owing to their faithlessness. Say, what a wicked course your faith has led you to, if indeed you are of the faithful.* (2:93)

The expression in this verse, *and their hearts became filled with the love of the calf* could literally be translated, "...and the love of the calf was drunk (*Ushribu*) into their hearts." It became strongly infused into their hearts via the conduit of their eyes. They stared adoringly at the golden calf and its love gradually overwhelmed their hearts. This illustrates the nature of the relationship between these conduits and our hearts. We must assiduously guard ourselves against the corrupting influences that surround us in this environment if we are to maintain a healthy heart.

The obligation governing smell follows that of hearing and vision. Everything that it is lawful for you to listen to or to look at, it is permissible for you to smell. It is related that some musk was brought to 'Umar bin 'Abdul 'Aziz. He pinched his nose. He was asked about that and replied, "Is it benefited from in any way other than its fragrance?"

He pinched his nose because the musk was illegally purchased and he did not want to smell something illicit. One might ask, "How can smelling something be considered forbidden?" Many of the things that are forbidden as types of filth are accompanied by foul odors. We could mention carrion, feces, urine, alcohol, tobacco, etc. Similarly, many carcinogens are known to emit foul odors, as anyone living in the vicinity of a refinery, or other industries known to produce carcinogenic waste can attest to.

On the other hand, the best things ever created are distinguished by their beautiful fragrances. Anas said:

I served the Messenger of God, peace upon him. He never uttered an expression of disapproval to me. He never asked, 'Why did you do this or why did you not do that?' I swear by God that I never touched any variety of silk softer than the hand of the Messenger of God, peace upon him. Nor did I ever smell any aroma or fragrance sweeter than the aroma and fragrance of the Messenger of God, peace upon him.[276]

The believer is given a good fragrance based on the righteous deeds he or she does. The Prophet, peace upon him, mentioned, "The likeness of the believer who regularly recites the Qur'an is like a citron, both its taste and fragrance are wonderful."[277] He also mentioned, "The likeness of the Qur'an and one who teaches it and acts on it is like a pouch filled with musk. Its fragrance diffuses everywhere."[278]

We should strive to be people whose fragrance defines them. By so doing we will be blessed to imbibe the incomparably sweet fragrance of Paradise, if God so wills.

The obligation of the hands and feet is that they are not extended towards something forbidden, and that they are never closed from engaging the truth. Masruq said, "No servant takes a single step except that it is recorded as a good or an evil deed." The daughter of Sulayman bin 'Abdul Malik wrote to 'Abdah the daughter of Khalid bin Ma'dan, asking that she visit her. 'Abdah wrote back, "My father used to dislike traveling anywhere that he could not guarantee before God as being for a lawful purpose, or to eat anything whose lawfulness he could not establish on the Day of Judgment. I dislike what my father disliked. Peace upon you."

To insure that we use our limbs in ways pleasing to God we have to do two things: First of all, we have to ensure that our hearts are pure and in tune with the divine law. The second thing we need to do is to strive to attain the special status of *Walaya*, or love and nearness to God. When we are in a relationship of love and nearness to God, He ensures that we use our limbs in ways that are pleasing to Him, ways that are consistent with the law He has revealed. God expresses this reality in a divine hadith:

> I declare war against anyone displaying enmity towards one I have befriended. My servant does not draw near to Me with anything more beloved to Me than the obligations I have imposed on him. Then he continues to draw near to Me with the voluntary acts until I love him. When I love him, I become the hearing he hears with, the vision he sees with, the hand he grasps with, and the feet that convey him. If he were to ask anything of Me I would surely grant it. And were he to seek My protection I would surely protect him.[279]

The meaning of His saying, "When I love him, I become the hearing he hears with, the vision he sees with..." is that He blesses the servant to use these faculties in ways that are pleasing to Him and consistent with His commandments and prohibitions.

If a questioner were to ask, "How can one attain such a degree of impeccability?" It should be said, "By adhering to the way of the righteous Imams, by studying the etiquettes of the sincere seekers of guidance through spiritual exertion, by being spiritually alert through consistent self-accounting, by being just in one's actions,

by adorning oneself by refraining from harming others, by sharing one's virtue while not reminding others of the good one has done for them, by having dignified comportment free from even a hint of jealousy, by being content through a love for anonymity, by remaining silent for extensive periods of time desiring to be safe, by being humble with people while not feeling cut off from their love, by finding intimacy with the remembrance of God in solitude, by freely serving others, by gathering all of your spiritual energy to be constantly vigilant, and by seeking salvation on the path of religious rectitude."

God, Mighty and Majestic, says in the Qur'an, Those who declare, Our Lord is God, and are thereafter consistently upright, fear will not overwhelm them nor will they grieve. (46:13) Sufyan bin 'Abdullah al-Thaqafi said, "O Messenger of God! Give me some guidance I can hold on to." He said, peace upon him, "Declare, I affirm my belief in God and thereafter be consistently upright."[280]

Uprightness and consistency in religion is a great characteristic. In his commentary on the hadith mentioned above, Ibn Rajab al-Hanbali mentions that being upright in religion involves both upholding divine oneness and consistent actions. Concerning divine oneness, he mentions:

One might say that what is intended by being upright in upholding divine oneness is adherence to a purified creed that makes the Hellfire forbidden for its possessor. It is the actualization of the meaning of, "There is no god but God" (La ilaha Illa Allah), for He is the deity that is obeyed. He is not rebelled against out of reverence, veneration, awe, hope, reliance, and seeking a favorable response to prayers. Sin in all of its various types undermines this unity for it involves responding to the call of the whimsical caller—Satan. God, Mighty and Majestic, mentions in the Qur'an, *Have you not seen one who takes his whims as his god?* (45:23)[281]

He then mentions concerning practice:

Uprightness is walking the straight path. It is the straight religion without deviating right or left. That includes undertaking all acts of obedience, both external and internal, and leaving all forbidden things.[282]

One who can consistently do what Imam Ibn Rajab has described here has attained to a great station in his or her spiritual growth, and God facilitates all success.

'Umar bin al-Khattab related, "They were consistently upright in their religion through obedience to God and they did not maneuver like a fox." Abu 'Aliya al-Riyahi mentioned, "Consistency means they were sincere in faith, prayer, and worship."

We cannot "maneuver like a fox" and expect to be consistent in our religion. "Maneuvering like a fox" means, looking for reasons to escape our religious responsibilities. It means making excuses for our shortcomings. It means justifying our transgressions. It means being inconsistent in our acts of obedience. All of these things involve a lack of sincerity.

The source of consistency lies in three things: Following the Qur'an, following the prophetic tradition, and adhering to the community of faith.

At the end of the day, Islam is simple. We have complicated it. If we adhere to the Qur'an and the prophetic tradition (*Sunnah*) by implementing what they convey to us of God's commandments, avoiding what they convey of His prohibitions, adorning ourselves with the etiquettes they lay out for us, and staying in the company of the people of truth we will do more for our souls than we will with years of empty philosophical speculation and inquiry.

The Prophet, peace upon him, summarized the simplicity of the religion when he mentioned, "The lawful is clear and the unlawful is clear. Between them are doubtful matters whose rulings many people do not know. Whoever avoids the doubtful matters escapes with his religion and honor intact."[283]

You should know that the surest path to salvation for the servant lies in acting on the basis of knowledge, allowing his fear to be a source of caution in religious matters, and being sufficed by God, Mighty and Majestic.

Knowledge is extremely important in Islamic teachings. God mentions, *Say, are they equal those who know and those who know not?* (39:9) The Prophet, peace upon him, was once asked about a devoted worshiper and a pious scholar. He replied, "The virtue of the pious scholar over the devoted worshiper is like the virtue of the full moon over all of the other heavenly bodies."[284]

This is so because it is knowledge that lights the path to Paradise. In our time of material advancement but spiritual poverty, those ignorant of the spiritual realities so crucial to the success of humanity belittle the sacred knowledge that is essential for salvation. Imam al-Marwardi expresses this situation beautifully in *Adab al-Dunya w' al-Din:*

Only the unthinking are ignorant of the virtue of knowledge. This is so because the virtue of knowledge is only known through knowledge. This [fact] only accentuates its virtue all the more for its virtue is only realized through its possession. When the unthinking lack the knowledge necessary to arrive at an understanding of its virtue, they naturally are ignorant of that virtue. They therefore debase its possessors and think that what their [own] souls incline towards of acquired wealth and prized novelties are justifiably striven for and more fitting to be preoccupied with.[285]

What Imam Marwardi mentions here is generally true in any area of endeavor. However, it is particularly true in the realm of sacred knowledge, for sacred knowledge is essential for the attainment of Paradise.

Therefore, work diligently to reform your state, acknowledge your need for your Lord, and rise above entertaining doubtful matters. Decrease your dependency on people, love for them what you love for yourself, and hate for them what you hate for yourself.

There is a general lesson being conveyed here that is applicable for all of the points the Imam mentions. Namely, do not waste your time for you will need all of it in striving to attain Paradise. Delving into doubtful matters is a great waste of time for such matters are usually involved and are thus amenable to extensive research, debate, and discussion. However, at the end of the day, they are not essential in terms of what we need to know to succeed in this life and the next. They are thus of no concern to us.

Similarly, over dependence on people leads to situations that result in us wasting our valuable time. We do not need what people possess, we need what God possesses. Our concern for people should be searching for ways to benefit them, for in benefiting them, we benefit our own souls. Hence, Imam al-Muhasibi's advice, *"...love for them what you love for yourself, and hate for them what you hate for yourself."*

If we love for them what we love for ourselves, we will spend our time trying to secure those things for them. Similarly, if we hate for them what we hate for ourselves, we will spend our time trying to ward those things off from them. The Prophet, peace upon him, mentioned in this regard, "No one of you truly believes until he loves for his brother what he loves for himself."[286] The good we would love for ourselves we should love to see accrue to others. When we internalize this hadith and act on its requisites, it will demand that we are a source of good, both to our own souls and to others.

Never consider any sin to be insignificant, never divulge a secret, never reveal what God has concealed, never contemplate committing a sin, and never persistently commit a minor transgression.

This advice is extremely relevant as many times we place ourselves in spiritual danger by having our hearts stained by numerous sins that we never bother to repent from because we deemed them insignificant. Another dangerous habit that afflicts many people is making it easy for themselves to fall into minor sins. One of the sages mentioned, "There are no minor sins if they are persistently engaged in and there are no major sins if they are eradicated by repentance."

Minor sins become major in two ways. First of all, if we consistently commit them we lose the fear of breeching the sanctity surrounding sin. At that point, we can easily fall into major sin because our sensitivity to the concept of sin itself has been eroded. Likewise, by persevering in minor sins we are taking the mercy of God for granted. That breech of etiquette with God oftentimes results in His removing His protection from us, and in an unprotected state, it becomes very easy for us to slip into major sins. One of the ways to avoid both pitfalls is by not allowing ourselves to be pulled into sins, be they major or minor, by cutting off the suggestion to sin before it grows into a conscious thought.

Imam al-Muhasibi discusses revealing secrets in the midst of this section. Some might deem this inclusion curious. However, one of the unsuspecting sins people fall into is revealing secrets. Imam Ghazali includes revealing secrets as one of the ruinations of the tongue. He mentions that the reason for this prohibition is that it "involves harming others, belittling the rights owed to knowledge and the rights of friends."[287] This is a serious issue that many people are oblivious of.

The Prophet, peace upon him, warned, "If a man speaks and then leaves that gathering, what he said is a sacred trust."[288] Luqman was asked, "How did you obtain to the virtue we observe in you?" He replied, "Truthful speech, conveying what I am entrusted with, and leaving what does not concern me."[289] We have to strive to guard the trust, for its breech not only undermines the integrity of Muslim society, it is also something that might lead its perpetrators to Hell.

Seek refuge in God during every time of need, acknowledge your need for Him in every situation, and rely on Him in every affair.

We are in constant need of God. Ibn 'Ata Allah mentions in his *Aphorisms*, "There are two indispensable blessings that every created thing is inescapably in need of: The blessing of being created, and the blessing of being sustained."[290] Were it not for these two great blessings nothing else would matter.

Only God can provide them. God declares in the Qur'an, *O People! You are in dire need of God, while God is free of all needs, worthy of all praise.* (35:15)

This verse emphasizes the essential need and weakness of humanity. Were it not for God we would have nothing and we would be nothing. Even though we allow our technological prowess to delude us into thinking we have power, when we stand helpless before natural disasters such as tsunamis, hurricanes, cyclones, tornados, floods, or earthquakes, the reality of our inherent weakness is driven home to us. God reminds us in the Qur'an, *The human has been created weak.* (4:28)

As opposed to our inherent weakness, the nature of God is that He is all powerful. He can create from nothing. He controls the winds, seas, tides, and other forces of nature. He can bring the earth back to life after its death. It is He who is totally independent of us. This only magnifies the extent of His generosity and grace in dealing with us for He gives freely to us despite the fact that He needs nothing from us. He only asks that we worship Him, for the benefit of our souls, not for His benefit. For this reason, He is worthy of the highest praise.

Isolate your whimsical inclinations.

One of the greatest ways to control our vain inclinations, or whims, is by isolating them. We do this by not following up on them. Alone, our whims are weak and insignificant. We strengthen them when we reinforce them with our intellect, or our hands, our feet, our eyes, or ears. It is only with these tools that they are able to act. Without them they can do nothing. We must realize this and enforce their isolation. When they are isolated, they die.

This process of isolation is rooted in the fear of God. God mentions in the Qur'an, *As for the one who fears the station of his*

Lord and guards his soul against its whims, Paradise will be his repose. (79:40) Fear in turn is rooted in the knowledge of God. For this reason, Imam al-Muhasibi, has introduced this section with a discussion of the fear of God and its ensuing states.

Do not be content to wait for good to come to you. Try to avoid being the center of attention. Constantly thank God and seek His forgiveness abundantly. Reflect on your thoughts, and prepare for tribulations with sound knowledge.

The lesson here is for us to be active in seeking good for our souls and in warding off evil. This requires knowledge. One of the most beneficial areas of knowledge in this regard is knowledge of the many ways we can do good for our souls. God reminds us of the many paths to good that He opens before us, and His willingness to accept whatever we do in pursuit of that good. He says for example, *Whatever good you do, surely God knows it.* (2:215) *Whoever does the smallest amount of good will see it.* (99:7) *Whoever does any righteous deed does so for the benefit of his soul.* (41:46)

The Prophet, peace upon him, mentioned in this regard, "Do not consider any good deed you may do insignificant, even if it is meeting your brother with a smiling face."[291] As Muslims we must be conveyors of good and that good should leave an indelible mark upon the societies we find ourselves in.

One of the best forms of knowledge we can have is knowledge of the nature of the world. One who knows the nature of the world knows it is the abode of trials and tribulations. God reminds us, *Blessed is the one who holds the Dominion in His hands, and He has power over all things. It is He who has created life and death in order to test you, which of you is best in deed, and He is the Almighty, the Forgiving.* (67:1)

CHAPTER EIGHT

Be deliberate in those situations that seem to demand haste. Have good etiquette in the presence of others. Do not become angry with people in defense of yourself. Become angry with yourself for the sake of God.

Imam al-Muhasibi renders us valuable advice here. First of all, he reminds us of the importance of being deliberate and judicious in our affairs. None of us could ever count the times we have fallen into sin owing to haste. The Prophet has stated, "Deliberateness is from God, and haste is from Satan."[292] God wants us to consider well our choices for as rational actors, and as believers, we will generally tend to do what is in the best interest of our souls. Satan realizes this. Therefore, he tries to incite us into hasty, ill-conceived actions. He knows many of these actions will not be characterized by either judiciousness or deliberateness. Hence, if we are not careful we will work against our salvation.

One of the times we are most prone to acting in ways that are pleasing to Satan is at the onset of our anger. Many an argument, fight, insult or slight has occurred at this time.

For that reason, the Prophet, peace upon him, once repeatedly admonished, "Do not become angry."[293] His advice should not be understood to mean that we should never become angry. As human beings, there are inevitably times when we will become angry. Oftentimes our anger is justified. His advice means that we should not act in a manner pleasing to Satan during the times of our anger. We are encouraged to control our action during these times and to suppress the anger itself. God describes the pious as, *Those who spend their wealth in easy and difficult times, suppress their anger, and pardon people. God loves those possessing inner excellence.* (3:134)

Do not respond to anyone's wickedness in kind.

We should never reciprocate wickedness with wickedness. One of the great principles of our law is expressed in the prophetic hadith, "There is no harm or reciprocating harm."[294] As wickedness is a source of harm, we should avoid reciprocating it. We should always seek to progress on the high road, the one less traveled. Some of the milestones demarcating that road have been mentioned previously, such as, "Join relations with those who cut them with you, give to those who deny you, and ignore those who oppress you."[295] These are the qualities that define a person of true faith.

Many times we feel that if we take such an approach we will be abused or taken advantage of. It is important for the believer to trust in God in these matters. God would never ask us to do anything that involves our harm. He works in ways that defy our cognitive and analytical powers. It is on the basis of His power that unexpected outcomes occur. This principle is beautifully illustrated in the Qur'an, *Good and evil are not equal. Respond with what is best. Unexpectedly, you will see one between whom you and he there was enmity become as it were an intimate friend.* (41:34)

Our limited powers and faculties lead us to think that responding to evil with kindness will lead to disastrous results. However, God is capable of all things, and He is certainly capable of turning people's hearts around. We merely need to display the courage needed to do our part. God is in control. He also mentions, in a verse that reinforces the meaning of the above one, *Is the reward for good ever anything other than good?* (55:60)

The purpose of this book is to cultivate in people the spiritual qualities necessary to walk on this path, for indeed, it is a path that requires a large degree of spiritual maturity. God mentions that this station, *Will only be attained by those possessing patience, it will only be attained by the possessors of a bounteous share.* (41:35) The bounteous share referred to here is of spiritual maturity and fortitude.

Beware of the praise the ignoramus heaps upon himself, and do not accept praise from others. Limit your laughter and avoid unnecessary joking.

The only people we should praise are those capable of responding to that praise with humility and a heightened awareness of their responsibility before God. An ignoramus lacks the proper knowledge to respond thus and hence should not be praised. He also does not realize the damage that praise can have on one's spiritual development, therefore he does not hesitate to praise himself.

As for ourselves, we should not accept the praise of others. We should not rebuke them for their words, unless they go beyond limits acceptable by the standards of both religion and civility. However, we should deflect that praise by rightfully saying, All Praise is for God (*Al-Hamdulillah*)."

One of the most profound statements of humility in the face of praise is that uttered by Imam 'Ali in *Nahj al-Balagha*:

He mentioned that if a God-conscious person is praised he responds:

> I know myself better than others do, and my Lord knows me better than I know myself. O God! Do not take me to task because of what they say; make me better than what they think of me; and forgive me for those things they do not know about me.[296]

Imam al-Muhasibi also warns us about excessive laughter in this passage. Excessive laughter is something that kills the heart. The Prophet, peace upon him, warned us, in the context of a lengthier hadith:

> Avoid forbidden things and you will be the most devout of people. Be content with what God has portioned out for you and you will be the wealthiest of people. Treat your neighbor well and you will be a true believer. Love for people what you love for yourself and you will be a true Muslim. Finally, avoid excessive laughter for excessive laughter kills the heart.[297]

He also warned against unnecessary joking. Like laughter, joking should not be excessive. However, just as there is a time and place for laughter there is a time and place for joking. Our Prophet, peace upon him, was human, and like all balanced human beings there were occasions when he joked around with his Companions. However, even in his light moments he would only speak the truth.[298] Hence, we should never lie to make a joke.

Here we will mention some of the jokes of the Prophet, peace upon him. It is related that an elderly lady came to the Prophet, peace upon him. He said to her, "An elderly lady will not enter Paradise." Hearing this she wept. The Prophet, peace upon him, then said, "At that time you will not be elderly." He then recited the Qur'anic verse, *We have created them in a unique and unprecedented way. We have made them pure virgins, full of love, sharing with them the same youthful age.* (56:35-37)[299] In Paradise, wives will be the same age as their young husbands.

In another narration, it is mentioned that a man came to the Prophet, peace upon him, and asked him for a ride on his camel." He responded, "I will give you a baby camel to ride." He said, "What am I going to do with a baby camel, it will not be able to carry me!" He replied, "There is no camel except that he is another camel's baby."[300]

Although there is clearly a place for laughter and light-heartedness in our religion, we should beware of being excessively jocular. We should never be far from the sobering thought of our death and the awesome realities that will accompany the Day of Resurrection. It is the lack of the knowledge of these realities that sometimes leads to our joviality. The Prophet, peace upon him, said, "If you knew what I knew you would laugh little and weep much."[301]

Hide your pain, be chaste, internalize trust, be aware of the inability of people to help you, let poverty be a form of protection, be patient in dealing with afflictions, be content with what God has allotted you, and be absolutely certain concerning God's promise and apprehensive of His threat.

A Muslim is a dignified, sober, strong, and self-reliant person. He does not complain of pain and injuries, but bears both with dignified grace. This was the way of the first generation. The Qur'an reminds us that charity *...is for the needy that are restricted in their ability to travel in the Way of God, and* *cannot traverse the earth. The ignorant think that they are rich owing to their disciplined restraint.* (2:273) This description is befitting the materially poor Companions, because they did not manifest their poverty, pains, and hardships. Even more than that, they were willing to allow others to take advantage of those things they themselves could have used to improve their situation. God says, *They give preference to others even though they themselves are poverty-stricken.* (59:9)

One of the reasons they so readily accepted poverty is because they realized that in many ways it is a blessing in disguise. When one is poor, one has less worldly attachments and is therefore freer to worship God. Likewise, poverty pushes away "friends" and acquaintances that are not sincere. People of such ilk see little to gain materially from a poor person and therefore do not seek them out. This also reduces their worldly attachments and helps to bring them sincere friends who are more likely to assist them as they move along the path to God. A poor person also has less to account for on the Day of Judgment.

Collectively, all of these things help a poor person to gain Paradise. Therefore, poverty is a protection of sorts for them from the fire of Hell. Saying this, we should mention that extreme poverty can also be factor leading a person to despair of God's Mercy, or to become obsessed with the world because of the intensity of his longing for the worldly things the wealthy possess.

There are some people whose faith is only sustained by wealth. In such cases, poverty may actually hasten their descent into Hell. Similarly, we have been taught by the Prophet, peace upon him, to seek refuge against poverty that will make us forget our duty to God. He said:

Are you waiting for poverty that will cause you to forget [your religious obligations]; or wealth that

will lead you to transgress; or disease that will de-
bilitate your body; or senility that will scramble your
thoughts; or a sudden death; or the emergence of the
Antichrist— and he is the most evil thing awaiting
you; or the coming of Doomsday? Doomsday is more
calamitous and bitterer.[302]

**Do not burden yourself with what has been guaranteed
you. Do not fall short pursuing what you have been
entrusted to seek. Acknowledge your need of everything
God blesses you with, and long for salvation from Him.**

We have not been burdened by God to guarantee our sustenance. He has assumed that responsibility. However, most
of us spend an overwhelming majority of our time pursuing
our livelihood. On the other hand, God has commanded us to
worship Him. Yet, we fall drastically short in performing that
basic duty. This irony has been captured by Ibn 'Ata Allah in
his *Aphorisms*. He says, "Your arduous assertion towards what
has been guaranteed you, and your laxity in what has been
demanded of you, is an indication that your inner light has
been extinguished."[303]

Both Imam al-Muhasibi, and Ibn 'Ata Allah are reminding us that we are in this world to worship God. We are not
here to neglect God while we pursue our whims and chase
after what has been guaranteed for us by God. We have to
make sure we are about our true business. That business is
worshipping God and serving our fellow humans.

**Pardon those who oppress you, and give to those who
deny you. For God's sake join relations with those who
cut you off, and give preference to those who love you
for His Sake. Freely extend your soul and your wealth**

to your brothers, and be careful to fulfill the religious
rights owed to your Lord.

We have already discussed these issues.[304]

**Do not consider any good deed you perform to be great,
nor any bad deed you perpetrate to be insignificant.
Beware of the hidden guiles of the heart. Surely, God
has numerous punishments.**

We have previously discussed these issues. In this context, Imam al-Muhasibi is using them to illustrate the guiles
of the heart. A beguiling heart is one that has been overwhelmed by its enemy—Satan. One of the greatest means
to prevent Satan from overwhelming our hearts is to know
the entrances he exploits to find a way into them. Imam
Ghazali has listed the most vulnerable of these entrances in,
The Revival of the Religious Sciences. We will list them some of
them here:

1. Anger and lustfulness.
2. Jealousy and avarice.
3. Overeating. This strengthens the carnal appetites
    which are the weapons of Satan.
4. Love of ostentatious furniture, clothing and houses.
5. Seeking to impress people.
6. Haste and inadequate preparation for tasks.
7. The love of money.
8. Stinginess and fear of poverty.
9. A fanatical defense of one's positions and opinions.
10. Novices engaging in the discussion of involved theo-
    logical issues.
11. A bad opinion of other Muslims.[305]

Once one has identified these entry points one has to immediately work to close them by leaving these characteristics. After closing them, one seals them shut by constantly remembering God through the various forms of His remembrance that are available—*Salat, Dhikr,* Qur'anic recitation, invocations, supplications, and other devotional acts.

Beware of dissemblance with your knowledge just as you are cautious not to become conceited with your actions. Do not think that some etiquette you have internalized cannot be nullified by conceit arising from knowledge.

Here, Imam al-Muhasibi mentions one of the most important etiquettes associated with knowledge. Namely, that one should try one's best to never show off or behave boastfully with ones knowledge. As we have mentioned earlier, knowledge is a sacred trust and a gift from God. It is not fitting that something given to an individual by God becomes something he then uses to show off with before his fellow humans. Sufficient warning against such a vile practice is found in the following words of the Prophet, peace upon him, "Whoever seeks knowledge to vanquish fools in debate, to vie with scholars, or to turn people's glances towards him, will be in Hell."[306]

Knowledge naturally stimulates arrogance in a person for he possesses something others lack. Therefore, it is especially important to make sure that we take every measure we can to humble ourselves as we travel the path of knowledge. One of the surest means to do this is by making sure that we choose teachers who themselves are humble. Imam Ghazali makes a powerful statement in, *The Revival of the Religious Sciences*, which every student should reflect on. He says that you should only sit with a scholar that calls you from five things to five things, "From doubt to certitude; from dissemblance to sincerity; from worldly longing to worldly abstinence; from arrogance to humility; and from enmity towards people to extending to them sincere advice."[307]

We should be mindful that even the refined aspects of our religious practice can be undermined by conceit and arrogance. These are qualities of Satan. When present in the human heart, owing to their vileness, and to the extent that they are hated by God, they can undermine less essential aspects of the religion such as the etiquettes associated with our external actions.

Obey God even if it means disobeying people, and never obey people if it means disobeying God, Most High.

Islam aims to create a social order that is qualified by a respect for the commandments and prohibitions of God. For that reason, obedience to God is placed over obedience to people. One of the signs of an Islamic social order is that people are discouraged from openly sinning. If certain sins are committed privately, they are not viewed as grave as those that are committed publicly. Private transgressions, while still being abominations before God, do not directly undermine the public order.

This orientation is rooted in the prophetic message. The Prophet, peace upon him, mentioned:

> Everyone in my nation will be forgiven except those who broadcast their sins. To broadcast one's sins includes a man committing a sinful act at night. He wakes up in the morning, finding God has concealed it. He then proclaims, "O so-and-so! Last night I did such-and- such!" He turns in at night and his Lord has concealed [his sin], and then he wakes up and removes God's concealment from himself.[308]

Further illustration of this idea is the saying of 'Umar bin 'Abd al-'Aziz, "God does not punish the general populace for sins committed privately. However, when sinning occurs openly everyone deserves punishment."[309]

Do not hold back anything from God in your devotional acts. Do not allow your soul to be pleased with an action that should have been undertaken solely for God. Stand before God in prayer with your entire being.

Here Imam al-Muhasibi is exhorting us to give ourselves totally to God. What we hold back may be the thing that gives Satan a foothold from which he can assault us. God links these two concepts in the Qur'an—total commitment, and the assault of Satan. He says, *O Believers! Enter into Islam completely and do not follow the footsteps of Satan. He is unto you a clear enemy.* (2:208)

Entering into Islam totally means two things. The first is to enter into it wholeheartedly with complete sincerity. The second is to accept all of its rulings, working to avoid picking and choosing based on our whims and preferences. To do otherwise, is to follow the footsteps of Satan. He rebelled against God based on the whimsical inclinations of his soul. This complete submission to God and His religion should in no place be more manifest than in the ritual prayer.

We should endeavor to constantly improve the quality of our prayer by perfecting our mastery of the rulings associated with it and by working to perfect our attentiveness and focus during it. This is something many people neglect to the detriment of their souls. The ritual prayer was described by the Prophet, peace upon him, as "the coolness of his eye."[310] This idiom means the delight of the soul. There is no greater means of spiritual elevation or jubilation than the prayer when properly performed with due attentiveness and focus.

CHAPTER NINE

Earnestly and energetically convey the obligatory poor due. Protect your fast from lying and backbiting.

Imam al-Muhasibi here mentions some of the etiquettes associated with the poor due (*Zakat*) and the fast. The poor due should be paid promptly and enthusiastically. This is a sign of our love for the poor, whom our Prophet, peace upon him loved, and our love for God, who has ordained that we spend of our wealth in this manner. It is also recognition that the wealth we have been blessed with is in reality not ours. God reminds us, *And give them from the wealth of God, which He has given you.* (24:33) By recognizing this reality, we readily spend our wealth, which is the greatest form of thankfulness we can give for it. Hence, it is one of the surest means to bring about its increase.

The Imam is also encouraging us to guard our fast by adhering to the etiquettes that are involved with the fasting person protecting his tongue. When these etiquettes are not observed, the fast loses its true essence—namely, that it is a means to God-consciousness. The Prophet, peace upon him, mentioned, "How many people fast and only end up getting hungry; and how many people spend the night in prayer and only end up missing sleep?"[311]

The destructiveness of backbiting for the fast is emphasized by a hadith related by Imam Ahmad:

> Two women fasted during the time of the Prophet, peace upon him. They nearly died of thirst. Their case was mentioned to the Prophet, peace upon him, and he turned away. When their situation was mentioned a second time, he summoned them and asked them to induce vomit. They vomited a bucketful of pus, blood and raw meat. The Prophet, peace upon him, said, "These two have fasted from what God has made lawful for them, and then broke their fast with what He has forbidden. They sat with each other and began eating the flesh of people."[312]

Carefully guard the rights of the neighbor, the poor, and the relative.

The Prophet, peace upon him, introduced a social code that placed great emphasis on the rights of the neighbor. Good treatment of neighbors has been made a part of faith. The Prophet, peace upon him, mentioned in that regard, "Whoever believes in God and the Last Day, let him treat his neighbor well."[313] Once the Prophet, peace upon him, repeatedly said, "I swear to God he does not believe!" It was said, "Who O Messenger of God?!" He replied, "One whose neighbor is not safe from his wickedness!"[314]

He also mentioned, "He is not a believer who satiates himself while his neighbor is hungry."[315] 'Abdullah bin 'Amr bin al-'As mentioned, "I heard the Prophet, peace upon him, refer to the Angel Gabriel, saying, 'He counseled me so frequently concerning the neighbor that I thought he would make him an heir.'"[316] Abu Dharr mentioned, "The Prophet, peace upon him, counseled me, 'O Abu Dharr! If you cook a broth add extra water to it and give some to your neighbors.'"[317] The ruling of this hadith pertains to anything one cooks that effuses a pleasant aroma. One has to see if one's neighbors are needy and if so one must share the dish with them.

These are just some of the Prophet's, peace upon him, teachings concerning the neighbor. We have to guard these rulings for they are an essential aspect of our religion and a part of its contribution to the legacy of human civilization.

The same is true for the poor and relatives. We must diligently guard their rights. Islam is a religion that encourages social responsibility, as we have mentioned above. God lets us know that the poor have a right to part of our wealth. He mentions in the Qur'an, *Charity is for the poor and the indigent…* (9:60) Likewise, *…and in their wealth is a well-known right, for the beggar and the deprived.* (70:24-25)

We are living in a world whose economic system is systematically marginalizing billions of people. We have a tremendous responsibility towards people who have been challenged by possessing far less material means than ourselves. One of the greatest tributes to the poor of the Muslim community is that they will accompany the Prophet, peace upon him, into Paradise. He said, "…He will enter me into Paradise along with the poor Muslims, and I do not say that boastfully."[318]

This attentiveness to the poor and less fortunate members of society is one of the hallmarks of our religion. It is the "steep path" that God encourages the believers to travel. He says, *And what will lead you to realize what the step path is? It is freeing the slave. It is providing food during a time of famine—to the*

*orphan who is related, or to the dust-covered indigent person. Only
then will he be of those who truly believe; those who counsel each other
with patience, who counsel each other with mercy.* (90:12-17)

Train your children, and treat your employees gently.

Our religion places great emphasis on the training of children. As humans we have not been left to wander aimlessly
through this life. It is incumbent upon the present generation to pass on to the coming generation those qualities we
have inherited from our ancestors that support our humanity.
That would include knowledge of God and His messengers,
culminating with our Prophet, Muhammad, peace upon him.
We have to teach our children to love God and His Messenger, peace upon them. We have to teach them the Qur'an, its
proper recitation and its language. We have to teach them the
obligatory acts of worship which they will be responsible to
undertake upon reaching adulthood. We have to teach them
the virtues and etiquettes a believer is expected to manifest.
This is perhaps the most daunting task we have before ourselves in these days where manners, civility, and an appreciation for proper comportment and decorum have been seriously
eroded.

One of the greatest characteristics parents can manifest
in dealing with children is gentleness. We have mentioned
the hadith in which Anas bin Malik, the young servant of
the Prophet, peace upon him, mentioned that he served
him for ten years, and he was never struck, rebuked or
admonished.[319]

The ability to be gentle and then to have that gentleness
appreciated is a blessing from God, especially in the context of
the family. The Prophet, peace upon him, once said to 'Aisha,
"O 'Aisha! Be gentle. When God desires good for the members
of a household He directs them to the gate of gentleness."[320]

Gentleness should extend to employees or anyone we have authority over as it is a fundamental principle of our religion, which like many others has been neglected. Among the prophetic traditions in this regard are the following:

"Gentleness is not found in anything except that it beautifies it, and it is not removed from anything expect that it defiles it."[321]

"One denied gentleness has been denied all good."[322]

"O God! Make things difficult for anyone abusing their authority, in any sphere, in order to make things difficult for my community, and be gentle with anyone in authority over them who treats them gently."[323]

Be upright for justice as your Lord has commanded you.

God commands in the Qur'an, *O Believers! Be upright for justice, witnesses for God; even if it is against yourselves, your parents, or your relatives; whether they are rich or poor...* (4:135) He likewise says, *O Believers! Be upright for God witnesses for justice, and do not allow your hatred of a people to cause you to swerve from the just course. Be just! That is closer to righteousness. Be mindful of God, for God is well-informed concerning all that you do.* (5:8)

God has commanded us with justice in the strongest terms, as these verses illustrate, and has ordained that we adhere to the highest standards of morality. Our commitment to these ideals is the greatest hope for humanity as we see the world pillaged and torn asunder by profiteering war mongers and unbridled capitalistic greed. It will take people totally committed to an opposing set of values to even begin to check the rapacious forces that have been loosed in our world.

If you are motivated to do some good hasten to it.

Opportunities to do good do not return once they have passed. Either we take advantage of them or we neglect them. If we habitually neglect them we will find that they become scarcer. This is not owing to the fact that they no longer exist. Rather, it is owing to the fact that we no longer see them. We see them with our heart-vision and our failure to take advantage of them leads to the dimming of that vision and the weakening of our ability to discern them. God mentions in the Qur'an, *It is not their eyes that are blinded. Rather, the hearts that are in their breasts.* (22:46) It is the blindness of the hearts that renders some people impervious to the warnings God sends them. It is the blindness of the hearts that causes them to ignore His signs, even though they are everywhere to be witnessed. It is the blindness of the hearts that causes them to miss the opportunities to do good, even though those opportunities are almost endless.

Hence, when we are motivated to do some good, we must seize the moment. We must act as expeditiously as we possibly can before we lose both our motivation and the opportunity. God urges us in the Qur'an, *Hasten to forgiveness from your Lord and a Paradise whose expanse rivals that of the heavens and earth. It has been prepared for the God-conscious.* (3:133)

If the religious ruling concerning something escapes you, leave it.

We should only act on a matter if we know its ruling. If we do not know its ruling we should leave it. In most instances such matters are not essential for our religious or worldly life. The things that are absolutely essential for our survival in this world and for our otherworldly salvation are clear. God has clarified and preserved the rulings in such matters. If we leave obscure matters it will not be a source of ruin for us.

In fact, as the Prophet, peace upon him, mentioned, if we leave such matters we "escape with our religion and our honor intact."[324]

Be merciful to the sinners, and never leave giving sincere counsel to the believers.

In many instances, sinners are not bad people. They have fallen into sin due to misguidance, error, or negligence. Hence, their turning away from sin requires someone to guide, correct, or remind them. The Prophet, peace upon him, performed all of these functions. As opposed to being people who berate, scorn or neglect sinners, we should be merciful to them and work to assist them in doing the things that will lead to their leaving their sinful behavior. This is a function of our giving sincere advice to the believers. Paradise, as mentioned in the previous verse, is expansive. We should work to assist as many people to enter it as we possibly can. One of the greatest means to assist us in this regard is mercy.

Speak the truth wherever you are. Do not make many oaths even if you are a truthful person. Do not argue, even if you are right. Beware of excessive speech, even if you are eloquent. And beware of ostentation [in religion], even if you are a scholar.

We cannot emphasize enough that the tongue is the part of our body that will lead us to transgress against others more than any other appendage or organ. The ruinations of the tongue are quite numerous. We have previously mentioned the importance of truthfulness. Here we will mention those instances when it is permissible to deviate from the exalted standard Islam demands. Imam Nawawi summarizes the Islamic teachings in this regard:

Speech is a means to obtain objectives. Lying is forbidden in the pursuit of any praiseworthy objective that can be obtained by the truth. If it can only be attained by lying, then lying is permissible. If the attainment of that objective is permissible then lying is permissible. If its attainment is obligatory then lying is obligatory.

Imam Nawawi then gives examples of this idea:

If a Muslim were hiding from an oppressor who was trying to kill him or usurp his wealth, and a person were asked concerning his whereabouts, it would be obligatory for him to lie in order to conceal his location. Similarly, if he had been entrusted to hold something for someone and an oppressor wanted to take it, it would be obligatory to lie to conceal it.

In such situations it is religiously more precautionary to use ambiguous language. That involves an expression whose intention is true, but whose obvious meaning, in the context the hearer understands, is false.[325]

Before we conclude that our religion is extending an open license to lie, we should be mindful of the gravity of the situations mentioned by Imam Nawawi above, by way of illustration. We should also note a hadith mentioned by Umm Kulthum, in which she states, "I only heard the Prophet, peace upon him, permit people to deviate from the truth in three circumstances: War; reforming relations between people; and the slight distortions of the truth engaged in between husbands and wives [to maintain domestic tranquilty]."[326]

Another area of dangerous speech we should avoid is taking oaths, or swearing by God that we will do such-and-such. As Imam Muhasibi mentions, this is something even honest people should avoid. If a person is a liar and constantly swears oaths in God's Name, then he will be lying in the Name of God. Many people carelessly or flippantly mention, for example, "I swear to God I will meet you tomorrow." In reality they know they will probably not make the meeting. If in fact that is the case, they have lied in God's Name. As for the truthful person who engages in such a practice, he will end up burdening himself with what he cannot bear.

Know the ruling concerning what you say before you speak.

We have previously discussed this idea of refraining from acting until you know the ruling of a particular act.[327] Here we will mention the implications of advising people erroneously in religious matters. A basic principle in Islam is that no one can bear the sins of another person. However, if we were to erroneously relate the ruling of a particular action, that had sinful implications, and someone acted on that advice, we would share in their sin. This is so because our erroneous advice, in this case, involves a blameworthy innovation that has no basis in prophetic guidance. The Prophet, peace upon him, stated, in that regard:

> Whoever introduces into Islam a good innovation, he will be given its reward, and the reward of everyone who acts on it, without any lessening of their reward in any way. And whoever introduces into Islam a bad innovation, its sin will fall on him, as will the sin of everyone who acts on it, without their sin being lessened in any way.[328]

Fear that your devotions will not be accepted after exerting yourself to the utmost in worship.

We should never assume that our devotional acts will be accepted. One reason for this is that actions are based on the intention accompanying them. None of us knows if our intention is totally acceptable. We assume that it is and we can proceed in our affair with peace of mind. However, at the end of the day, God, who knows the hidden and the manifest, knows best. Hence, we should never take it for granted that our actions are acceptable.

Another reason is that piety is a condition for the acceptability of our actions. God mentions in the Qur'an, *Rather, God only accepts from the pious.* (5:27) Who amongst us would be so pretentious as to describe himself or herself as pious before God? It is related that Imam 'Ali said, "Be more concerned with the acceptability of your action than you are with the action itself. Have you not heard, *Rather, God only accepts from the pious.*" (5:27)[329] Fadala bin 'Ubayd mentioned, "If I knew that God accepted even a mustard seed of my actions that would be more beloved to me than the world and everything in it, for God has said, *Rather, God only accepts from the pious.*" (5:27)[330]

This understanding should not discourage us from working and striving to the utmost of our ability to do our very best in our devotional acts. Nor should it cause us to despair of God's mercy. It should help us to maintain a humble stance before our Lord and to constantly work to refine our intentions and actions.

Accommodate people as long as you do not compromise your religion by so doing, and avoid hypocrisy in all situations. Treat people with good character, and do not be too shy to say, "God knows best," concerning something you lack knowledge of.

We should not exalt ourselves above others nor see ourselves as being too good to mingle with the poor and downtrodden masses. This is one of the beautiful aspects of our religion; it forces us to interact with people from all social classes. In the congregational prayer we do not know, nor can we control, if we are standing next to a prince or a pauper. The same is true of the Hajj. To ensure harmonious relations with the many types and classes of people that the religion facilitates us dealing with we should try our best to accommodate people and to meet them at their level. This is essential for us if we wish to be good ambassadors for Islam. However, in so doing we should avoid hypocrisy, being two-faced and engaging in unjustified compromises.

Along these lines, we should visit relatives, maintain contacts with old friends, and try to maintain an air of conviviality with our neighbors, coworkers and fellow students. Such contacts create the openings to show people, first and foremost through our character, what Islam is truly about. These are the arenas where we can best follow the prophetic guidance, "Deal with people on the basis of good character."[331]

One of the ways we manifest good character is responding to people who ask us something we are ignorant of by saying, "I do not know." How many times have we asked someone for directions and they sent us on a "wild goose chase." Think of how wonderful it would have been if they had simply replied, "I'm sorry, but I do not know how to get there." Such an answer is one of the greatest displays of good character for it embodies both truthfulness and humility.

IMAM AL-MUHASIBI'S CONCLUSION

What follows is the final section of Imam al-Muhasibi's *Risala*. Most of the themes he discusses below have been commented on in the previous chapters of the book. Any further commentary on my part would involve a lot of redundancy. I have also ended my commentary here in order to allow the reader to enjoy the uninterrupted flow of Imam al-Muhasibi's ideas. Linguistically, this final section is probably the most eloquent in the book. This only adds to the power of his words. Although not a formal conclusion in the original text, I feel that this section fittingly summarizes what the Imam has mentioned earlier.

Do not impose yourself verbally on someone not interested in what you have to say, and do not impose your religious values on one who will use them as a means to justify hating you. Do not expose yourself to tribulations you do not have the strength to bear. Consider yourself too noble to allow anyone to humiliate you. Allow your spiritual aspirations to exalt you above base character. Only take a trustworthy person as your brother in religion.

Do not reveal your secrets to everyone. Do not give a person more credit than he deserves, do not speak to him at a level he cannot comprehend, and do not enter into an affair without justification.

Reverence the gatherings of the scholars, know the value of spiritual sages, and never fail to recompense any good that is done for you, even if the only means you have to do so is prayer.

Turn away from ignoramuses. Patiently endure the imprudence of fools. Seek the counsel of those who fear God. Help your brother when he is oppressed, and turn him back to the path of truth when he is an oppressor. Fully extend to him the rights you owe him, while foregoing the rights he owes you. Be lenient with one indebted to you, and be gentle in your treatment of widows and orphans. Honor those who endure poverty with patient dignity. Be merciful to wealthy people who have been exposed to tribulation. Never envy anyone for a blessing, and never backbite anyone.

Close the door to your entertaining a bad opinion of others by fearing the responsibility [before God for that], and open the door leading to a good opinion of others by interpreting their actions in the most gracious manner. Shut the door to greed by realizing people can ultimately offer you nothing, and seek to open the door to true wealth with contentment.

Exalt God's mention by not attributing calamities to Him. Profit from your time, and realize how much of it is wasted by night and by day. Constantly repent to God. Divide your lifetime into three parts: A third for seeking knowledge, a third for worship, and a third for dealing with your rights and responsibilities.

Consider well those who have gone before you, and reflect on the fate of the two parties that will stand before God, Most High: A party that will be in Heaven owing to His pleasure, and a party in the blazing inferno of Hell having incurred His anger.

Know just how close God is to you, and honor the noble angels recording your every deed. Receive the blessings of God by trying to understand the wisdom behind them, and respond to them by praising God and thanking Him in the very best manner.

Beware of your soul causing you to imagine spiritual stations for yourself that you have not attained, or holding the truth to be foolishness by demeaning people. Both of these are deadly poison. Avoid fearing that you will fall from the esteem of people, by fearing that God will hate you for that. Avoid the fear of poverty by realizing just how close the expiration of your lifespan is.

Hide the evidence of your good deeds to the extent possible. Exert yourself when giving counsel. Be resolute in loving for the sake of God, and be decisive in breaking relations for His sake. Only befriend righteous people, only sit in the circles of scholars, and only keep the company of intelligent, spiritual people. Follow the way of the scholars who preceded you, and be a sincere teacher of the Muslims who will come after you, a leader for the righteous, and a refuge for the seekers of guidance. Do not openly complain to anyone, and do not allow your worldly affairs to consume your religion.

Take your fair share of isolation. Only eat from the lawful, avoid waste, and be content with what suffices you from the world. Seek etiquette in the orchards of knowledge, intimacy in the realms of isolation, shyness in the paths of certitude, contemplation in the valleys of reflection, and wisdom in the gardens of fear.

Know the constancy of God's grace to you despite your constantly opposing His commandments, His forbearance with you despite your neglecting His remembrance, His veiling your faults despite the paucity of your shyness before Him, and His absolute independence from you, despite your absolute need of Him.

Where is one who truly knows his Lord? Where is one truly fearful of his sins? Where is one truly happy with His nearness? Where is one truly occupied with His remembrance? Where is one truly fearful of being distant from Him? He is the one who forgives you, O deceived one! Does the Most Majestic not see you, while you have discarded the veiling {of your sins}.

You should know, my brother, that sinning leads to heedlessness, heedlessness leads to hardness of heart, hardness of heart leads to being distant from God, and being distant from God leads to Hell. Rather those who are spiritually alive reflect on this. As for the spiritually dead, they have murdered their souls with the love of the world.

Know that just as a person lacking vision cannot benefit from daylight, similarly, only the righteous can be illuminated by the light of knowledge. Just as a dead person cannot benefit from medicine, likewise, good etiquette cannot benefit those who claim unmerited spiritual stations. Just as a downpour will not cause anything to grow on a solid rock, likewise, wisdom will not emerge from a heart in love with the world.

One comfortable with his whims will have little etiquette. One who opposes the orientation of his knowledge will be exceedingly ignorant. One who has not benefited from his own medicine cannot treat others. Know that the most relaxed people are those with the least worldly concerns. They are the true ascetics. The most stressed people are those with the worldliest preoccupations. They are those obsessed with the world.

The characteristic that is most helpful in attaining true asceticism is abandoning the expectation of a long life. The most accessible state of the gnostics is thinking of the time one will stand before God. God says, *Surely, God ever watches over you.* (4:1) Know that there is no path more accessible than truthfulness, no guide surer than knowledge, and no provision more beneficial than piety.

I have found nothing stronger in negating the whisper of Satan than abandoning excess. Nothing gives more illumination to the heart than a magnanimous spirit. I have found the nobility of a believer to lie in his piety, his forbearance in his patience, his intellect in his effort to beautify himself, his love in his ability to overlook and pardon others, and his honor in his humility and gentleness.

Know that loving wealth when God has chosen poverty for His servant incurs divine wrath, while loving poverty when God has blessed His servant with wealth is tyranny. Each state involves fleeing away from thankfulness, owing to a lack of spiritual insight, and a waste of time owing to a paucity of knowledge.

This is so because the faith of a rich person will not be sound in the face of poverty, while the faith of a poor person will not be sound in the face of wealth. This is expressed in the divine hadith, "Verily, among my servants is one whose faith is only rectified by poverty, were I to enrich him that would ruin him. While among them is one whose faith is only rectified by wealth, were I to impoverish him that would ruin him."³³² The same is true for health and illness.

One who knows God does not blame him. One who understands God is pleased with His decree. If people of knowledge only knew the following verse it would suffice them: *Your Lord creates what He desires and He chooses. They have no choice.* (28:68)

Beware of the characteristics of the ignorant, the gatherings of sinners, the false claims of the conceited, the false hopes of the self-deceived, and the despair of the hopeless. Act on the truth, trust in God, command good and forbid wrong. God guides one who is truthful with Him. He disgraces one who adorns himself for other than Him. He suffices one who relies on Him. He hates one who trusts in other than Him. He grants security to one who fears Him. He gives increase to one who thanks Him. He honors one who obeys Him. He loves one who prefers Him. One beloved by his Lord is victorious.

Beware of intellectualizing faith, acting on your whims, leaving the truth, acknowledging falsehood, and then seeking forgiveness while failing to repent. You should know that no knowledge or action is pleasing [to God] except that whose foundation is rooted in certitude, whose branches are elevated by truthfulness, whose fruits grow in impeccability, whose proof is established in fear, and whose secrets are veiled by reverence. Do not be content with a half-hearted effort for there is no excuse for shortcomings, and no one is free of God.

Know that the happiness of a person lies in his having a good intention to obtain what God, Most High, alone possesses, and being given the facilitation to attain His love. When God desires good for anyone He blesses him with a sound intellect, makes knowledge beloved to him, bestows fear [of God] on him, makes gentleness his way, enriches him with contentment, and shows him his faults.

You should know, may God have mercy on you, that truthfulness and sincerity are the foundations of every state. Patience, contentment, true asceticism, pleasure, and intimacy are branches of truthfulness. While sincerity branches out into certitude, fear, love, majesty, shyness, and magnifying [God]. Each believer has a place in one of these stations, which he passes, and which then is the state he is known by.

Hence, it is said of him, fearful, yet he has hope; or hopeful, but he has fear; patient, but he has satisfaction; loving, but he has shyness. The strength or weakness of every state is proportionate to the faith and gnosis of the servant.

The foundation of each of these states has three signs by which it is known. Truthfulness is in three things, which are not complete without it: Truthfulness of the heart in faith that is actualized; truthfulness of intention in religious actions; and truthfulness of expression in speech.

Patience is in three things, which are not complete without it: Patience in avoiding those things God has forbidden; patience in [dealing with the difficulty involved in] following the command of God; and patience at the time of a calamity, while anticipating God's grace. Contentment is in three things, which are not complete without it: [Being content with] little materially even though material means are available; with deprivation when possessing nothing and the prospects of future abundance are lacking; and with the tranquility found in the worship of God, Mighty and Majestic, despite being steeped in poverty.

Contentment has a beginning and an end. Its beginning lies in abandoning excessiveness despite the existence of plenty. Its end is the existence of spiritual wealth despite material poverty and lack of worldly means. From this point of departure, one of the sages mentioned that contentment is a higher station than satisfaction. What he meant is complete contentment, because the state of one who is satisfied does not change according to his being denied or given. One who is content is enriched with his Lord. He does not seek any increase along with Him to assuage the desire of his soul—unless that increase is a gift from God to him.

Abstinence is in three things, the ascetic is not called abstinent without them: Ridding himself of worldly possessions; passing up enjoyment of some lawful things; and being carefree because of the large amounts of time [devoted to God]. A man is a true ascetic if he is characterized by three other things: He protects his soul when tempted by his desires; he flees from opportunities to enrich himself materially; he only meets his needs with what he knows to be lawful.

Intimacy is in three things: Being intimate with sacred knowledge and remembrance of God during spiritual retreat; being intimate with certitude and gnosis during spiritual retreat; being intimate with God in every state.

Satisfaction is in three things: [Satisfaction with] the rulings of God, Mighty and Majestic; submitting to His command; and not to seek alternatives to His decree. Satisfaction is the buttress of love, the soul of reliance [on God], and the very spirit of certitude. It has been related from Ayyub al-Sakhtiyani and Fudayl bin 'Iyad that they used to say, "Satisfaction is reliance."

These are branches of truthfulness that are taken from the attributes of knowledge. Sufyan al-Thawri, the Mercy of God upon him, used to say, "When the honesty of the truthful is complete, he knows that he does not own anything."

As for the branches of sincerity, a sincere person is not known by that name until he absolves God from any likeness, equal, consort, or children. Then the object of his desire is only God resulting from pure monotheism. He then focuses all of his concerns on Him and for Him in every obligatory and voluntary action.

The soundness of certitude is in three things: the heart finding total comfort trusting God; being led by the command of God; and fear and apprehension concerning God's Preordained Knowledge.

Certitude has a beginning and an end. Its beginning is inner peace, and its end is being sufficed by God alone. This is consistent with His saying, Mighty and Majestic, *Does not God suffice His servant?* (39:36) Likewise, *O Prophet! Sufficient for you is God and those who follow you of the believers.* (8:64) Sufficiency is through He who suffices and the sufficed is the servant who is satisfied with what God, Most High, has degreed.

We have said that the end of certitude is found among the attributes of the servant in the station of faith; and it is not associated in this sense with knowledge. {Were it situated} in knowledge no one would ever comprehend it. This is reflected in the saying of the Prophet, peace upon him, "No one will ever comprehend the essence of God." They said, "O Messenger of God! It has reached us that Jesus walked on water." He is reported to have then said, peace upon him, "If his certitude and faith had been increased he would have walked in midair."[333]

Fear can only exist after certitude. Have you ever seen anyone afraid of something he is not certain of? Fear is in three things: The fear involved with true faith. Its sign is diligently striving to abandon rebellion and sin. This is the fear of those seeking God.

[There is] the fear of Salb. Its signs are reverence, apprehension, and scrupulousness. This is the fear of those who know God. [Then there is] the fear of Fawt. Its signs are diligent exertion in seeking the pleasure of God accompanied by awe and veneration. This is the fear of those who uphold the truth of the prophetic call.

A fourth station[334] of fear is specifically relevant to the angels and the prophets, peace upon them. It is the fear of magnification, which is present despite the fact that both are safe owing to the protection He has extended to them. Their fear in this regard is a function of their worship of God, out of awe and veneration.

Love is in three things. The lover is not called a lover without them. [They are]: Loving the believers for the sake of God—the signs of that are refraining from harming them, and securing benefit for them as it is known in the law brought by Muhammad.

[Then there is] the love of the Messenger, peace upon him. The signs of that are following his way. God mentions, may His remembrance be magnified, *Say, if indeed you love God follow me; then God will love you...* (3:31)

The love of God, Mighty and Majestic, is in preferring obedience over sinful rebellion. It is said that remembering the blessings encourages love. Love has a beginning, middle, and an end. Its beginning lies in loving God for His blessings and favors. Ibn Mas'ud related, "Hearts have been naturally oriented to love those who treat them well."[335] Who is better than God, the Clement, and the Generous, in fulfilling an oath, demonstrating mercy and compassion, and overlooking faults?

Its middle is implementing His commandments, avoiding the things He has prohibited, such that He never finds you passing up something He has commanded you to undertake, and He never finds you involved in something He has forbidden. If you fall into sin, you immediately confess that sin and turn away from it.

Its epitome is in loving God because it is a binding right owed to Him. 'Ali bin Fudayl mentioned, "God is loved because He is God."

A man came to Tawus and said, "Advise me." Tawus said:

> I advise you to love God so deeply that nothing is more beloved to you than Him; that you fear Him until there is nothing more feared by you than Him; that you long for His mercy so intensely that it prevents that fear from overwhelming you; and that you love for other people what you love for yourself. Now stand up and leave for I have summarized for you the knowledge of the Torah, the Gospels, the Psalms and the Qur'an.

Furthermore, you should know that veneration and exaltation are related to each other as the head is related to the body. One cannot do without the other. If a servant is shy before his Lord he exalts and venerates Him. The source of shyness is constant mindfulness of God's surveillance. Mindfulness of God's surveillance is in three things: being mindful of it during worship thereby dutifully undertaking the acts of obedience; being mindful of it while engaged in sinful rebellion thereby ceasing it; and being mindful of it in one's conscious and subconscious thoughts. This is as the Prophet, peace upon him, said, "Worship God as if you see Him and if you fail to see Him, know that verily He observes you"[336] Awareness of God's surveillance is more fatiguing to a servant than the hardships involved in regularly standing for prayer at night, perpetually fasting, and spending in the way of God.

It is related that Imam 'Ali bin Abi Talib used to say, "God has placed vessels in the earth, and among those vessels are hearts. He only accepts hearts that are pure, strong, yet soft."[337] This means that a heart being pure for God lies in implementing His commandments and avoiding His prohibitions along with the witness of truthfulness and apprehension.

Its purity for the Messenger of God, peace upon him, lies in accepting what he has brought, with our speech, actions, and intentions. Its purity for the believers lies in refraining from harming them and securing benefit for them. As for his saying, "...strong," this means that it is strong when implementing the divinely proscribed punishments, commanding right, and forbidding wrong. As for his saying, "...soft," this softness is twofold: softness displayed by weeping, and softness displayed by compassion.

It is God who facilitates all success. He suffices us, what an excellent trustee!

GLOSSARY

Badr The name of the location of a spring where the first major battle undertaken by the Prophet Muhammad, peace upon him, and his Companions occurred.

Dhikr The conscious remembrance of God. Usually associated with the recitation of litanies and invocations, the term has a wider meaning that encompasses recitation of the Qur'an, studying sacred knowledge, and other actions that preoccupy the tongue and the heart from worldly concerns.

Divine Hadith A saying directly revealed to the Prophet Muhammad, peace upon him, from God. However, it differs from the Qur'an in that the choice of words is that of the Prophet, peace upon him; whereas the Qur'an is a direct revelation, and it embodies the eternal speech of God.

Duha The early part of the day that extends from just after sunrise until the sun reaches its zenith. It is the time of the post-sunrise prayer that bears it name.

Fajr The latter part of the night that extends from the crack of dawn until the beginning of the sunrise. It is the time of the obligatory prayer that bears its name.

Ghayb The unseen realm of existing metaphysical reality, and the realm of yet to be manifested physical reality.

Gnosis The experienced knowledge of God.

Hadith The recorded sayings, actions, agreements, and descriptions of the Prophet Muhammad, peace upon him.

Hajj The annual Muslim pilgrimage to Mecca. It reaches its culmination during the twelfth month of the lunar calendar, *Dhul Hijjah*, with the gathering of the pilgrims on Mount Arafat.

Heart-vision The inner vision of a spiritually sound heart. It allows its possessor to see the underlying reality of things and the more subtle manifestations of God's names and attributes in the world.

Hijab The religiously mandated covering of the Muslim woman. This is sometimes limited to a description of the scarf used to cover her hair and neck. It has also been used to refer to such covering as a symbol of femininity and its attendant modesty.

Ihsan Inner excellence or the highest level of religious refinement. It is ultimately the description of a state of awareness of God's surveillance of His servants' actions; as the Prophet, peace upon him, described it as, "Worshipping God as if you see him."

Ijma' Legal consensus or agreement. It involves the collective agreement of scholars who have obtained the rank of independent juridical reasoning during a particular era, on the ruling of a specific legal issue, after the death of the Prophet, peace upon him.

'Ilm al-Kalam Speculative or dialectic theology as developed by Muslim scholars. Its essence involves using logical proofs to substantiate theological truths.

Iman Faith or belief. It involves the sincere acceptance and affirmation of the existence of God and the ensuing details of creed and practice as made known through His Prophets, peace upon them, culminating with the mission and message of the Prophet Muhammad, peace upon him.

Islam The proper name for the religion sent by God to guide humanity. It also refers to the actual practice of that religion.

Istidraj An apparent blessing, given to a corrupt person, which is in reality a cause for his/her ruin.

Janazah The body of a deceased person after its preparation for burial. More generally, it refers to the funeral rites of Islam.

Jihad al-Nafs The struggle against the guiles and treachery of the unrefined soul or ego.

Ka'bah The cubical-shaped structure located in the Sacred Mosque in Mecca, faced by Muslims during the ritual prayer.

Mecca An ancient, sacred city near the Western coast of the Arabian Peninsula. It is the location of the Sacred Mosque, the Ka'bah, and the birthplace of the Prophet Muhammad, peace upon him.

Medina A sacred city located to the north of Mecca. It was the place that the Prophet Muhammad, peace upon him, migrated to in order to establish the first capital of an identifiable Muslim polity.

Moral Psychology A modern discipline dealing with the study of the psychological bases for moral action.

Mu'tazilites The rationalists. A major Islamic sect who based their creed, legal philosophy and worldview on the primacy of human reasoning, giving preference to reason in instances where divine revelation apparently clashes with human reason.

Mutakallim A practitioner of speculative or dialectical theology. Usually identified as a theologian adhering to the Sunni theological schools established by Abu al-Hasan al-Ash'ari or Abu al-Mansur al-Maturidi.

Nasiha Offering sincere advice to other humans in interpersonal relations, and being sincerely faithful to God, His messenger, and His scripture.

Qadarites An early Islamic sect, arising within the school of the rationalists. They denied the effect of God's decree on human actions. The advocates of uncensored free will.

Qur'an God's eternal, uncreated speech directly revealed to the Prophet Muhammad, peace upon him, and recorded in compilations referred to as *Musahif.*

Quraysh The Arab tribe to which the Prophet Muhammad, peace upon him, belonged, and his staunchest enemies until their entrance into Islam.

Rububiyya The Lordship of God. It is a term that describes his exclusive and unrestricted ability to act in His creation.

Salat The ritual prayer of the Muslims, containing bodily, mental, and spiritual elements. It begins with the extolling of God's greatness (*takbir*) and culminates with the conveyance of peace (*taslim*).

Shari'ah The divine law revealed by God through the Qur'an and the Prophet Muhammad, peace upon him. Its immediate application, based on rulings derived by human reasoning and understanding, is referred to as *Fiqh*.

Sirat The bridge traversing Hell. It will convey the believers into Paradise.

Sunnah The confirmed way or tradition of the Prophet Muhammad, peace upon him. As one of the legal values in the Islamic ethical scheme, it refers to highly desirable actions.

Taqwa God-consciousness that leads to a willingness to obey God's commandments and to avoid His prohibitions.

Tarawih The nighttime supererogatory congregational prayer that is performed during the month of Ramadan.

Tasawwuf (Sufism) The science of Islamic spirituality and moral psychology. It focuses on inculcating into the believer the constant remembrance of God, awareness of the afterlife, the identification and eradication of negative character traits, and the adoption of virtuous ones.

Uhud The name of a hill on the outskirts of Medina that was the scene of the second major battle involving the Prophet Muhammad, peace upon him, his Companions, and the Quraysh.

Uluhiyya/Ilahiyya A term referring to the exclusive right to worship that is owed to God.

Ummah The collective community of the Prophet Muhammad, peace upon him. The *Ummah* can be divided into the Community Being Invited (*Ummah al-Dawah*), and the Community of Respondents (*Ummah al-Istijabah*), which is comprised of those who actually profess Islam. The former group includes all of humanity from the time of the passing of the Prophet Muhammad, peace upon him, until the Day of Judgment.

Walayah A status of friendship and nearness to God that He bestows upon the select of His righteous servants. Only God knows who is afforded this status. However, any righteous, pious, obedient servant is eligible for selection.

Zuhd Worldly abstinence or the process of divorcing the heart from worldly attachments and distractions. This process can be completed even if the servant is wealthy, as long as the heart is not overwhelmed by preoccupation with that wealth. Hence, it has nothing to do with wealth or poverty.

ENDNOTES

1 Imam Muslim bin al-Hajjaj, *Sahih Muslim* (Beirut: Dar Ihya' al-Turath al-'Arabi, 1420/2000), no. 2956.

2 There are varying dates mentioned for the founding of Basra. The date we mention here, 14H/635AD, is based on the account of Yaqut al-Hamawi. See Imam Shihab al-Din Yaqut bin 'Abdullah al-Hamawi, *Mu'jam al-Buldan* (Beirut: Dar Ihya al-Turath al-'Arabi, 1417/1997), 2:342.

3 Hasan al-Basri was born , 21H/642AD.

4 H.A.R. Gibb and J.H. Kramers, eds., *Shorter Encyclopaedia of Islam* (Ithaca: Cornell University Press, 1953), 136.

5 Harun al-Rashid died 193H/809AD.

6 See Muhammad Bek al-Khudari, *al-Dawla al-'Abbasiyya* (Beirut: Mu'assasa al-Kutub al-Thiqafiyya, 1415/1995), 131.

7 Imam Taj al-Din al-Subki discusses this issue in his biography of Imam al-Muhasibi. Although Imam al-Muhasibi was a younger contemporary of Imam al-Shafi'i, the narrations that mention any relationship between Imam al-Muhasibi and Imam al-Shafi'i do not seem to clearly indicate that Imam al-Muhasibi was an immediate student of Imam al-Shafi'i. However, there is no doubt that he did adopt Imam al-Shafi'i's school. See Taj al-Din al-Subki, *Tabqat al-Shafi'iyya al-Kubra*, ed. 'Abd al-Fattah Muhammad al-Jalu (Cairo: Dar Ihya al-Kutub al-'Arabiyya, n.d.), 2:275.

8 It is reported that Imam Ahmad once secretly attended one of the lessons of al-Muhasibi and wept until he passed

out. He subsequently praised al-Muhasibi and his followers. However, he did not recommend that one of his own
students join al-Muhasibi's circle. This incident is summarized by Imam Ibn Hajar al-'Asqalani, in his entry on al-
Muhasibi in *Tahdhib al-Tahdhib*. Imam Ibn Hajar opines
that Imam Ahmad made that recommendation owing to
the loftiness of the state of al-Muhasibi and his followers. See, Imam Ibn Hajar al-'Asqalani, *Tahdhib al-Tahdhib*,
ed. Khalil Ma'mun Shiha, et al. (Beirut: Dar al-Ma'rifa:
1417/1996), 1:464.

9   For details related to the lives of these individuals see Zayn
al-Din Muhammad al-Munawi, *al-Kawkab al-Duriyya fi
Tarajim al-Sadah al-Sufiyya*, ed. Adib al-Jadir (Beirut: Dar
al-Sadir, 1420/1999).

10 Al-Muhasibi's intellectual prowess is summarized by 'Abdul-Qadir bin Tahir al-Tamimi who mentions: "He is the
Imam of the Muslims in jurisprudence, Sufism, hadith,
and theology." See Munawi, 1:586.

11 This incident is related by Abu Nu'aym in, Imam Abu
Nu'aym Ahmad bin 'Abdullah al-Asfahani, *Hilya al-Awl-
iya wa Tabaqat al-Asfiya* (Beirut: Dar al-Fikr, 1416/1996),
10:75.

12 For an overview of some of the aspects that define al-Muhasibi's moral psychology, and examples from his writings, see Michael Sells, *Early Islamic Mysticism: Sufi, Qur'an,
Mi'raj, Poetic, and Theological Writings* (New York: Paulist
Press, 1996), 171-195.

13 For a full discussion of al-Muhasibi's conceptualization of
divine grace and its role in the life of a believer see Mar-
garet Smith, *An Early Mystic of Baghdad: A Study of the Life
and Teachings of Harith B. Asad al-Muhasibi* (London: The
Sheldon Press, 1935), 178-182.

14 Imam al-Harith al-Muhasibi, *Kitab al-Tawwahum*, ed. Muhammad 'Uthman al-Khasht (Cairo: Maktaba al-Qur'an, n.d.).

15 Imam Harith al-Muhasibi, *Adab al-Nufus*, ed. Muhammad 'Abdul-'Aziz Ahmad (Cairo: Maktaba al-Qur'an, n.d.).

16 Imam al-Harith al-Muhasibi, *Kitab al-Nasa'ih*, ed. Muhammad 'Abdul-'Aziz Ahmad (Cairo: Maktaba al-Qur'an, n.d.).

17 Imam al-Harith al-Muhasibi, *al-Ri'aya li Huquqillah*, ed. Dr. Abdul Halim Mahmud (Cairo: Dar al-Ma'arif, n.d.).

18 Imam Abu Talib al-Makki, *Qut al-Qulub*, ed. Sa'id Nasib Makarim (Beirut: Dar Al-Sadir, 1416/1995).

19 Imam Abu Hamid al-Ghazali, *Ihya 'Ulum al-Din* (Beirut: Dar al-Qutayba, 1412/1996).

20 Imam al-Harith al-Muhasibi, *Risala al-Mustarshidin*, ed. Shaykh 'Abd al-Fattah Abu Ghudda (Aleppo: Maktab al-Matbu'at al-Islamiyya, 1416/1995).

21 Abd al-Rahman bin Muhammad al-Najdi al-Hanbali, *Majmu' al-Fatawa Shaykh al-Islam Ahmad bin Taymiyya* (Riyadh: Dar al-'Alam al-Kutub, 1412/1991), 10:455-549.

22 Al-Najdi al-Hanbali, 10:91-149.

23 Imam ibn Qayyim al-Jawziyya, *Kitab al-Ruh*, ed. Yusuf 'Ali Budaywi (Damscus: Dar Ibn Kathir, 1422/2002).

24 Imam Ibn Qayyim al-Jawziyya, *Madarij al-Salikin*, ed. Bashir Muhammad 'Uyun (Damascus: Maktaba Dar al-Bayan, 1420/1999).

25 Imam Ibn Rajab al-Hanbali, *Lata'if al-Ma'arif fi ma li Mawasim al-'Amm min al-Wadha'if*, ed. Ya Sin Muhammad al-Sawas (Damascus: Dar Ibn Kathir, 1416/1996).

26 Imam Ibn Rajab al-Hanbali, *Jami' al-'Ulum w'al-Hikam*, ed. Shu'ayb al-Arna'ut, et al. (Beirut: Mu'assasa al-Risala, 1414/1994).

27 Muslim, no. 8.

28 All of these sayings are quoted in Munawi, 586-588.

29 Imam Ahmad bin Hanbal, *al-Musnad*, ed. Shu'ayb al-Arna'ut, et al. (Beirut: Mu'assasa al-Risala, 1420/1999), no. 1477.

30 It is as if he is saying that his remorse is already established with God.

31 The word employed by Imam al-Muhasibi here for "Pre-existing" is "al-Qadim." Contemporarily, many scholars opine that the use of this term is a blameworthy innovation as it has no basis in the transmitted evidence that creedal positions are to be based on. However, closer examination reveals that this is not the case. Imam Hakim relates a hadith in his *Mustadrak* that lists "al-Qadim" (the Preexisting) among the names of God. See Imam Abu 'Abdullah Muhammad al-Hakim al-Nisaburi, *al-Mustadrak 'ala al-Sahihayn*, ed. Mustafa 'Abdul-Qadir 'Ata (Beirut: Dar al-Kutub al-'Ilmiyya, 1411/1990), no.42. Additionally, Abu Dawud mentions a hadith in his compilation where the Prophet, peace upon him, supplicated, "I seek refuge with God Almighty, with His noble face, and His Preexisting, Authoritative Power (*Sultanihi al-Qadim*), from the accursed Satan." As God's authoritative power is inseparable from His essence, both are fitting qualified as "Qadim." See Imam Abu Dawud Sulayman bin al-Ash'ath al-Sajistani, *Sunan Abu Dawud* (Riyadh: Dar al-Salam 1420/1999), 78, no. 466. Although Imam Hakim's narration is weak, the fact that this term was circulating among the scholars of hadith in narrations going back to the earliest generations of Muslims, long before the theological schools were consolidated, indicates that it was not an innovation introduced later on by the speculative theologians. Surely, God knows best.

32 Imam Abu 'Isa Muhammad bin 'Isa al-Tirmidhi, *Jami'*
    Imam al-Tirmidhi (Riyadh: Dar al-Salam) 1420/1999), no.
    2329.

33 See Imam Fakhruddin Razi's explanation of this verse. He
    expounds on the thoughts we summarized here. Imam
    Fakhruddin al-Razi, *Tafsir al-Razi* (Beirut: Dar 'Ihya
    al-Turath al-'Arabi, 1417/1997), 4:349.

34 Imam Abu 'Adbullah Muhammad bin Yazid ibn Majah,
    Sunan Ibn Majah (Riyadh: Dar al-Salam) 1420/1999), no.
    2043.

35 Imam Abu 'Abdullah Ahmad bin Hanbal, *Musnad Imam
    Ahmad*, ed. Shu'ayb al-Arna'ut, et, al. (Beirut: Mu'assasah
    al-Risala, 1420/1999), 28:367, no. 17.142. Tirmidhi, no.
    2676. The expression, "...bite into them with your hind
    teeth" means cling to them with all of your might.

36 The command "Say!" in the Qur'an is usually addressed to
    the Prophet, peace upon him.

37 Tirmidhi, no. 2676.

38 Quoted in Imam Muwaffaq al-Din 'Abdullah bin Ahmad
    bin Qudamah, *al-'Itiqad*, ed. 'Adil 'Abd al-Mun'im Abu
    al-'Abbas (Cairo: Maktaba al-Qur'an, n.d.), 23.

39 ;Ibn Majah, no. 3793, Tirmidhi, no. 3375.

40 Imam Abu Ja'far al-Tahawi, *The Creed of Imam al-Tahawi*,
    trans. Hamza Yusuf (Berkeley, CA: The Zaytuna Insti-
    tute, 2007) 56.

41 Thomas Hobbes, *Leviathan*, (London: Penguin Classics,
    1982) 186.

42 Imam Abu 'Abdullah Muhammad bin Isma'il
    al-Bukhari, *Sahih al-Bukhari* (Beirut: al-Maktaba al-'Asri-
    yya, 1426/2005), 27, no. 52; Muslim, no. 1599.

43 Bukhari, no. 1, Muslim, no. 1907.

44 Muslim, no. 2564.

45 Shaykh 'Abd al-Majid al-Shurnubi, *Sharh al-Hikam al-'Ata'iyya* (Damascus: Dar Ibn Kathir, 1413/1992), no. 22.

46 Tirmidhi, 560, no. 2459.

47 This refers to the time when we will stand before God for judgment.

48 Muslim, no. 2684.

49 Muslim, no. 2807.

50 Imam Abu al-Hasan 'Ali bin Muhammad al-Mawardi, *Adab al-Dunya w' al-Din* (Damascus: Dar Ibn Kathir, 1415/1995) 115-116.

51 Ibid., 117.

52 Ibid., 118.

53 Imam Abu Dawud Sulayman bin al-Ash'ath al-Sajistani, *Sunan Abu Dawud* (Riyadh: Dar al-Salam) 1420/1999), no. 3656.

54 Bukhari, no. 1152; Muslim no. 1159.

55 Andrew Delbanco, *The Death of Satan: How Americans Have Lost the Sense of Evil* (New York: Farrar, Straus & Giroux, 1996).

56 Tirmidhi, 3502.

57 Ibn Majah, no. 4105.

58 Bukhari, no. 6475; Muslim, no. 47.

59 Tirmidhi, 2317.

60 Ibn Rajab, 1:289.

61 Al-Shurnubi, no.4.

62 Quoted in Imam Ibn Hajar al-'Asqalani, *al-Isti'dad li Yawm al-Ma'ad* (Beirut: Maktaba al-Ma'arif, n.d.) 17.

63 Tirmidhi, no. 68.

64 Muslim, no.2012.

65 This incident is related in the biography of Imam al-Shafi'i in the introduction of *Kitab al-Umm* (Dar al-Fikr, 1403/1983), 9-10.

66 Tirmidhi, no. 2396.

67 Tirmidhi, no. 2398.

68 Al-Shurnubi, no. 8.

69 One could reflect on the message of Al-Qur'an 3:140, to ascertain the veracity of this statement. In this verse God mentions, *"These varying fortunes {victory, defeat; strength, weakness; influence, impotence} we alternate between people. This is in order that God shows who truly believes, and that He takes from your ranks martyrs. And God loves not oppressors."*

70 The influence of Comtean positivism was especially strong in 19th Century Egypt. Its influence on Muhammad 'Abduh is undeniable. Abduh wedded that positivism to his effort to create what he viewed as a viable Islamic worldview, along with a viable political and social morality. Abduh then influenced a generation of Islamist thinkers, most importantly Rashid Rida. Through them, positivist thinking became one of the distinguishing features of the 20th Century Islamic movement. For an indication of Comte's influence on 'Abduh see Albert Hourani, *Arabic Thought in the Liberal Age 1798-1939*, (Cambridge: Cambridge University Press, 2003) pp. 138-140.

71 Al-Shurnubi, no. 24.

72 Al-Qur'an 29:3. In this verse, God says, concerning the tests of this world, *"In order that God will show which of you are truthful, and which of you are liars."*

73 At-Tirmidhi no. 2396.

74 The crushing pain which afflicted the Messenger of God, peace upon him, occurred during his final illness. At-Tirmidhi, no. 2397.

75 Tirmidhi, no. 3382.

76 Imam Abu 'Abdullah Muhammad bin 'Abdullah al-Hakim al-Nisaburi, *al-Mustadrak 'ala al-Sahihayn*, ed. Mustafa 'Abdul Qadir 'Ata (Beirut: Dar al-Kutub al-'Ilmiyya, 1411/1990), 1:500, no. 1290.

77 Ibn Hisham, 92.

78 Bukhari, no. 6502.

79 Tirmidhi, no. 2516.

80 Tirmidhi, no. 2317.

81 Imam Ibn Juzayy al-Kalbi, *al-Tashil li 'Ulum al-Tanzil* (Beirut: Dar al-Arqam, n.d.), 1:69.

82 Tirmidhi, no. 2516.

83 Quoted in Ibn Rajab, *Jami' 'Ulum*, 2:108.

84 Tirmidhi, no. 3443.

85 Muslim, no. 91.

86 Muslim, no. 55.

87 Al-Shurnubi, no. 5.

88 God knows best as to the origin of this narration.

89 Imam Ahmad bin al-Husayn al-Ramli, *Safwa al-Zubad*, ed. Ahmad Jasim al-Muhammad (Jeddah: Dar al-Minhaj, 1426/2005), 50.

90 Tirmidhi, no. 2378.

91 'Abdullah bin Salam, who was a prominent Jewish authority in Medina, mentioned that when the Prophet, peace upon him, first entered the city he went to see him. As soon as his noble face became clearly visible he knew "his face was not the face of a liar." He accepted Islam shortly thereafter. See Tirmidhi, no. 2485.

92 Bukhari, no. 6574; Muslim, nos. 47, 74.

93 Bukhari, no. 6408; Muslim, no. 2689.

94 Muslim, no. 2588.

95 See Imam Ibn Qayyim al-Jawziyya, *al-Wabil al-Sayyab*, ed. Basir Muhammad 'Uyun (Beirut: Maktaba al-Mua'yyad, 1409/1989), 84-85.

96 Ibn Qayyim al-Jawziyya, *Zad al-Ma'ad fi Hadyi Khayri al'Ibad*, ed. 'Irfan 'Abd al-Qadir al-'Asha (Beirut: Dar al-Fikr, 1415/1995), 1:316.

97 Bukhari, no. 13; Muslim, 45.

98 Muslim, no. 55.

99 See Ibn Rajab al-Hanbali, *Jami' al-'Ulum w'al-Hikam*, 1:217-225.

100 Bukhari, no. 6094; Muslim, no. 2607.

101 Muhammad Zakariyya al-Kandahlawi, *Awjaz al-Masalik ila Muwatta al-Imam Malik* (Damascus: Dar al-Qalam1424/2003), 17:507, no. 1800.

102 Bukhari, no. 43.

103 Tirmidhi, no. 2333.

104 Imam Abu Hamid al-Ghazali, *Ihya 'Ulum al-Din* (Beirut: Dar al-Qutayba, 1412/1996), 4:651-790.

105 Tirmidhi, no. 2307.

106 Al-Ghazali, 4:653-654.

107 Cf. page 60-61.

108 I did not originate this parable. I once read it, but cannot recall where. However, I felt it was appropriate to mention it here.

109 Muslim, no. 2577.

110 Bukhari, no. 2448.

111 Cf. pages 16-17, 40-41.

112 Bukhari, no. 893; Muslim, no. 1829.

113 Mawardi, 11.

114 Yusuf 'Ali, summarizing what has been stated in a number of commentaries mentions these four issues. I have expanded on what he mentions slightly. See A. Yusuf 'Ali, *The Holy Qur'an: Text, Translation and Commentary* (New York: McGregor & Werner, 1946), 1653.

115 It is said by some that this expression is a hadith. Imam al-Ghazali mentions it in the *Ihya* (4:615) as a hadith, as does Imam al-Qurtubi, see Imam Abu 'Abdullah Muhammad bin Ahmad al-Qurtubi, *al-Jami' li Ahkam al-Qur'an* (Beirut: Dar al-Fikr, 1407/1987), 4:314. However, Ibn Jawzi mentions it as a fabricated narration in *al-Mawdu'at*. I have decided to mention it as a saying

that is not rightfully attributed to the Prophet, peace upon him. God knows best.

116   Imam Jalal al-Din al-Suyuti, *al-Jami' al-Saghir*, ed. 'Abduallah al-Darwish (Damascus: 'Abdullah al-Darwish, 1417/1997), no. 3358.

117   Ibn Majah, no. 4105.

118   Bukhari, no. 3209.

119   Muslim, no. 2585.

120   Al-Ghazali, 3:176.

121   Tirmidhi, no. 1995.

122   Tirmidhi, no. 1993.

123   Al-Ghazali, 3:177.

124   Tahawi, 58.

125   Ibn Qudamah, 22.

126   Imam Ahmad al-Rifa'i, *al-Burhan al-Mu'ayyad*, ed. 'Abd al-Ghani Nakahmi (Aleppo: Dar al-Kitab al-Nafis, n.d.) 17.

127   Shaykh As'ad Muhammad Sa'id al-Saghirji, *al-Jidd fi al-Suluk ila Malik al-Muluk* (Damscus: Dar al-Kalim al-Tayyib, 1422/2001), 374.

128   Bukhari, no. 6116.

129   Ahmad, no. 17985.

130   Tirmidhi, no. 2191.

131   Muslim, no. 8.

132   Abu Dawud, no. 2478.

133   Abu Dawud, 4807.

134   Tirmidhi, no. 2012.

135   Bukhari, no. 1585.

136   Imam Abu Ja'far Muhammad bin Jarir al-Tabari, *Jami' al-Bayan fi Ta'wil al-Qur'an* (Beirut: Dal al-Kutub al-'Ilmiyya, 1418/1997), 12:680, no.37879.

137   Bukhari, no. 6412.

138   Imam Abu Zakariyya Yahya bin Sharaf al-Nawawi, *Riyadh al-Salihin* (Beirut: Dar al-Jil, 1405/1985), 2.

139 Bukhari, no. 6416.

140 Muslim, 2807.

141 Bukhari, no. 1423.

142 Imam Abu al-Fida' Isma'il bin Kathir, *Tafsir al-Qur'an al-'Adhim* (Beirut: al-Maktaba al-'Asriyya, 1416/1996), 2:190.

143 Imam 'Ali bin Muhammad al-Jurjani, *al-Ta'rifat* (Beirut: Dar al-Kitab al-'Arabi, 1413/1992), 320, no. 1592.

144 Imam Abu Bakr Ahmad bin al-Husayn al-Bayhaqi, *Kitab al-Zuhd al-Kabir*, ed. Shaykh 'Amir Ahmad Haydar (Beirut: Dar al-Janan, 1408/1987), no. 343. This version of Imam Bayhaqi is weak. However, there are other narrations of the hadith that strengthen its acceptability. See Isma'il bin Muhammad al-'Ajluni, *Kash al-Khafa' wa Muzil al-Ilbas* (Beirut: Dar Ihya' al-Turath al-'Arabi, 1351/1929), 1:143, no. 412.

145 Cf. pages 29, 49-50.

146 We have discusses this hadith in the previous note. Cf. note 115.

147 Imam Abu Muhammad al-Husayn al-Baghawi, *Sharh al-Sunnah*, ed. Shaykh 'Ali Muhammad Mu'awwad, et al. (Beirut: Dar al-Kutub al-'Ilmiyya, 1412/1992), 1:185, no. 104.

148 Munawi, 1:572.

149 This particular saying is attributed to Muhammad bin Sirrin. See Muslim, p. 51.

150 Ahmad, no. 18001.

151 Imam Abu 'Abdullah Ahmad bin Hanbal, *Kitab al-Zuhd* (Cairo: Dar al-Dayyan lil-Turath, 1412/1992), 366.

152 Imam Abu Bakr Ahmad bin al-Husayn al-Bayhaqi, *Shu'ab al-Iman*, ed. Muhammad Sa'id bin Basyuni Zaghlul (Beirut: Dar al-Kutub al-'Ilmiyya, 1410/1990), 1:397-398, no. 528.

153 For a full examination of this concept see Dr. Sayyid Husayn al-'Affani, *al-Jaza' min Jins al-'Amal* (Cairo: Maktaba ibn Taymiyya, 1417/1996).

154 Our helping God is helping His religion or helping the people He loves. God is free of all needs worthy of all praise. Hence, He needs no help.

155 Al-Shurnubi, no. 8.

156 Tirmidhi, no. 2518.

157 Bukhari, no. 2442.

158 Abu Dawud, no. 4084; Tirmidhi, no. 2722.

159 Ahmad al-Rifa'i, 28.

160 Muslim, 51.

161 See Taqi al-Din Ahmad ibn Taymiyya, *al-Siyasa al-Shar'iyya* (Beirut: Dar al-Afaq al-Jadida, 1403/1983).

162 Cf. note 142.

163 Ibn Rajab, *Jami 'Ulum*, 1:364 What Ibn Rajab mentions at the end of this passage deserves our attention. When anger becomes the key factor in determining what we hold to be lawful or unlawful, then we are its servant and are guilt of a type of idolatry.

164 Quoted in Salih bin 'Abdullah bin Humayd, et al., *Nadra al-Na'im fi Makarim Akhlaq al-Rasul al-Karim* (Jedda: Dar al-Wasila, 1420/2000), 6:2443.

165 See Bukhari, no. 1423; Muslim, no. 1031.

166 Ahmad bin Muhammad ibn 'Ajiba al-Hasani, *Iqadh al-Himam* (Cairo: Matba' Mustafa al-Babi al-Halabi wa Awladuhu, 1381/1961), 39-42.

167 Imam Raghib al-Asfahani, *Mufradat Alfadh al-Qur'an*, ed. Safwan 'Adnan Dawudi (Damascus: Dar al-Qalam, 1423/2002), 461.

168 Bukhari, no. 4837; Muslim, no. 2820.

169 Ahmad, *Musnad*, no.21548.

170 Tirmidhi, no. 1987.

171 Ibn Rajab al-Hanbali, *Jami' Ulum w'al Hikam*, 1:482.

172 Bukhari, no. 1162.

173 Cf. pages 75.

174 Al-Shurnubi, no. 2.

175 Muslim, no. 1015; Tirmidhi, no. 2989.

176 Al-Munawi, 1:572.

177 Abu Dawud, no. 4918.

178 Shaykh Muhyiddin 'Abdul Hamid mentions these verses in his commentary on *Qatr al-Nada*. See Ibn Hisham, 100.

179 Tirmidhi, no. 2378.

180 Ahmad, *Musnad*, no. 17334.

181 Muslim, no. 2588.

182 These terms will be defined subsequently by Ibn Juzayy.

183 Ibn Juzayy, 1:176-177.

184 Imam Fakhruddin Razi, *al-Tafsir al-Kabir* (Beirut: Dar Ihya' al-Turath al-'Arabi, 1415/1995), 10:531.

185 Bukhari, no. 6094; Muslim, no. 2607.

186 Tirmidhi, no. 3127.

187 Imam Jalal al-Din al-Suyuti, *al-Jami' al-Saghir*, no. 8387.

188 Al-Shurnubi, no. 27.

189 Proverbs, 1:7.

190 A. Yusuf 'Ali, 161.

191 Al-Shurnubi, no 15.

192 Al-Jurjani, no. 453.

193 Tirmidhi, no. 2517.

194 Cf. note pp. 104-105.

195 Bukhari, no. 3116.

196 Abu Nu'aym, 6:95. Abu Nu'aym's version of the hadith contains an addition not mentioned by Imam al-Muhasibi. The lengthier version states, "Learn certainty as well as you learn the Qur'an. Verily, I am learning it.

197 Ibn Majah, no. 4102.

198   Cf. page 41.

199   Muslim, no. 2588.

200   Muslim, no. 91.

201   Muslim, no. 1015; Tirmidhi, no. 2989.

202   Abu Nu'aym, 10:15 Many people mention this narration as a prophetic hadith. However, Abu Nu'aym explains why it is more accurately related as a saying attributed to Jesus. He mentions it is unlikely that Imam Ahmad related this narration as a prophetic hadith. God knows best.

203   Qurtubi:2: 282.

204   Bayhaqi, *Shu'ab al-Iman*, no. 2439.

205   Shamsuddin Abu 'Abdullah Muhammad bin Tayyib al-Fasi, *Sharh Hizb Imam al-Nawawi*, ed. Bassam 'Abd al-Wahhab al-Jabi (Beirut: Dar al-Imam Muslim, 1408/1988), 55.

206   Ahmad, 2/381.

207   Bukhari, no. 71; Muslim, no. 1037.

208   Tirmidhi, no. 1987.

209   Tirmidhi, no. 1162.

210   Abu Dawud, no. 4700.

211   Abu Dawud, no. 4798.

212   Muslim, no. 2553.

213   Tirmidhi, no. 2004.

214   Tirmidhi, no. 2002.

215   Bukhari, no. 1.

216   Bukhari, no. 24; Muslim, no. 32.

217   Bukhari, no. 6117; Muslim, no. 37.

218   Bukhari, no. 6102; Muslim, no. 2320.

219   Quoted in Ibn Rajab, *Jami' al-'Ulum*, 1:501.

220   Bukhari, 43; Muslim, no. 785.

221   Muslim, no. 38.

222   Bukhari, no. 6570.

223   Ibn Hibban, no. 1971.

224 Quoted in ibn Rajab, *Jami' al-'Ulum*, no. 1:408.

225 Bukhari, no. 6416.

226 Salih bin 'Abdullah bin Humayd, 8:3617.

227 Hakim, no. 314.

228 Bukhari, no. 7281.

229 Muslim, no. 8.

230 Bukhari, no. 2887.

231 Tirmidhi, no. 2317.

232 Abu Dawud, no. 125.

233 Ibn 'Ajiba, 10.

234 Bukhari, no. 1423; Muslim, no. 1031.

235 Muslim, no. 2733.

236 Quoted in Ibn Hajar al-'Asqalani, *al-Isti'dad*, 22-23.

237 Bukhari, no. 1903.

238 Muslim, no. 1599.

239 Imam al-Muhasibi literally mentions "body" here. However, the passage is logically sounder if we read "heart." God knows best.

240 Ibn Hisham, 150.

241 Tirmidhi, no. 2459.

242 Ibn Majah, no. 4114.

243 Bukhari, no. 2887.

244 Ibn Majah, no. 1081

245 Ghazali, 4:7.

246 Ibn Rajab, *Jami' al-'Ulum w'al-Hikam*, 1:211.

247 Tirmidhi, no. 3407.

248 Bukhari, no. 2707.

249 Abu Dawud, no. 5073.

250 Bukhari, no. 7405; Muslim, no. 2675.

251 Imam Muhammad bin 'Ali al-Shawkani, *Tuhfa al-Dhakirin* (Beirut: Dar al-Ma'rifa, 1413/1992), 12.

252 Ahmad, *Musnad*, no. 22299.

253 Bukhari, no. 3336.

254   Imam Ibn Hajar al-ʿAsqalani, *Fath al-Bari* (Damascus: Dar al-Fayha', 1418/1997), 6:446.

255   The origin of this expression is unknown. God knows best concerning its authenticity.

256   Tabari, 12:684, no. 37914-37961б.

257   Muslim, no. 2408.

258   Muslim, nos. 763.

259   Literally, "...between his two jaws."

260   Bukhari, no. 6474.

261   Tirmidhi, no. 2616.

262   Bukhari, no. 6477.

263   See Ghazali, 3:169-239.

264   Imam Ghazali attributes this expression to Ibn Masʿud. See Ghazali, 3:172.

265   Abu Nuʿaym, 8:160.

266   Hakim, no. 7875.

267   Muslim, no. 2657.

268   Tirmidhi, no. 1639.

269   Tirmidhi, no. 3570.

270   This saying is actually a confirmed prophetic hadith. See Tirmidhi, no. 2777.

271   Imam Jalal al-Din al-Suyuti, *Lubab al-Nuqul fi Asbab al-Nuzul* (Beirut: Dar al-Maʿrifa, 1418/1997), 58.

272   Tirmidhi, no. 3353.

273   Muslim, no. 2564.

274   Cf. page 80.

275   Bukhari, no. 2412.

276   Imam Abu Muhammad ʿAbdullah bin ʿAbd al-Rahman al-Darimi, *Sunan al-Darimi* (Beirut: Dar al-Kutub al-ʿIlmiyya, 1417/1996), no. 62.

277   Ibn Majah, no. 214.

278   Ibn Majah, no. 217.

279   Bukhari, no. 6502.

280 Muslim, no. 38.

281 Ibn Rajab, 1:509.

282 Ibn Rajab, 1:510.

283 Muslim, no. 1099.

284 Abu Dawud, no. 3641.

285 Mawardi, 49.

286 Bukhari, no. 13; Muslim, no. 45.

287 Ghazali, 3:192.

288 Abu Dawud, no. 4868.

289 Kandahlawi, 17:501-502, no. 1798.

290 Al-Shurnubi, no. 97.

291 Abu Dawud, no. 4084.

292 Tirmidhi, no. 2012.

293 Bukhari, no. 6116.

294 Ibn Majah, no. 2341.

295 Cf. note 190.

296 Imam 'Ali bin Abu Talib, *Nahj al-Balagha* (Beirut: Mu'assasah al-'Ala lil-Matbu'at, 1424/2003), 416.

297 Tirmidhi, 2305.

298 Tirmidhi, 1990.

299 Imam Abu 'Isa Muhammad bin 'Isa al-Tirmidhi, *al-Shama'il al-Muhammadiyya*, ed. 'Abd al-Majid Ta'ma Halabi (Beirut: Dar al-Ma'rifa, 1417/1996), no. 250.

300 Abu Dawud, no. 4998.

301 Bukhari, no. 4621; Muslim, no. 2359.

302 Tirmidhi, no. 2306.

303 Al-Shurnubi, no. 5.

304 Cf. page 110-111.

305 Ghazali, 3:50-57.

306 Ibn Majah, no. 253.

307 Ghazali, 1:93.

308 Bukhari, 6069.

309 Quoted in Salih bin 'Abdullah bin Hamid et al., 11:5552.

310 Nasa'i, no. 3391.

311 Ahmad, no. 9685.

312 Ahmad, no. 23653.

313 Muslim, no. 47.

314 Bukhari, no. 6016.

315 Ahmad, no. 390.

316 Ahmad, no. 6496.

317 Muslim, no. 2625.

318 Tirmidhi, no. 3616.

319 Cf. page 178-179.

320 Ahmad, no. 24734.

321 Muslim, no. 2594.

322 Muslim, no. 2592.

323 Muslim, no. 1828.

324 Bukhari, no. 52; Muslim, 1599.

325 Nawawi, 328-329.

326 Muslim, no. 2605.

327 Cf. pages 91, 98, 150, 153, 206, 209.

328 Muslim, no. 1017.

329 Ibn Rajab al-Hanbali, *Lata'if al-Ma'arif*, 375.

330 Ibid., 375.

331 Tirmidhi, 1987.

332 Quoted in Ibn Rajab al-Hanbali, *Jami' al-'Ulum*, 2:332-333

333 This is apparently a fabricated narration that is best not attributed to the Prophet, peace upon him. Its origin seems to be in a tradition related by Ibn Abi al-Dunya, from Bakr bin 'Abdullah al-Muzani, who mentions a similar saying from Jesus, peace upon him.

Imam al-Khatib comments on this saying, which is narrated here by Imam al-Muhasibi, and repeated by Imam al-Ghazali in *The Revival of the Religious Sciences*. See Ghazali, 4:142, note 152.

334   The three are the fear involved with faith, the fear of *salb* and the fear of *fawt*.

335   Abu Nu'aym, 4:121. Abu Nu'aym relates this saying as a prophetic hadith. However, Imam al-Muhasibi seems to be correct in attributing it to Ibn Mas'ud.

336   Muslim, no. 8.

337   Suyuti, *al-Jami' al-Saghir*, no. 2390.

Made in the USA
Lexington, KY
08 February 2017